Praying During A
Pandemic
....After This

Linda D. Law

C.L.J.P.
Creative Unity Publishing

Praying During A Pandemic ...After This

Copyright © 2020 by Linda D. Law

ISBN 978-1-949402-12-4

Cover Design: Donna Osborn Clark at CreationsByDonna@gmail.com

Layout and Interior Design: www.CreationByDonna.com

Editing: Timothy G. Green at Inkaissance: inkaissance@gmail.com

Author photo by: Charles Beason Photography at www.charlesbeason.net

Published by: Creative Unity Publishing www.CreativeUnityPublishing.net

Scripture quotations used in this book are from THE HOLY BIBLE, King James Version, KJV from www.BibleGateway.com

Manufactured in the United States of America

First Edition

I dedicate this book to my family and to those that have inspired me to go further in God and in prayer. I dedicate it to those that have loved me enough, as well as to those who have hated me enough, to cause me to have to intensify my prayer life and take it to another level. This pandemic, that's happening right now as I type, has pushed me to write. I'm writing the book in the middle of a crisis situation. I'm writing in the midst of a "shut down" and I'm also writing out of pure obedience. I pray that this will help generations to come to fight in prayer and win. I'm writing for my children and my children's children and many, many generations ahead. I leave it as a legacy…

Introduction

I am inspired in this season to write and encourage during this pandemic. Corona Virus/Covid-19 "slipped" its way in to our world and it has caused many of us to reevaluate every area of our lives. I'm also inspired by a statement Bishop T.T. Hill of Tifton Georgia made passionately during a live online bible study. He said, "In order for the church to get to its rightful place and thereby cause the spirit of Jezebel to be annihilated throughout the body of Christ, we must come with a high praise and an intensified prayer."

This book is written for those that don't mind using warfare prayers that have been downloaded to me by way of the Holy Spirit. My prayer life has been developed through spending time with God, developing a relationship with Him and then allowing Him to direct me on what to say and how to say it through prayer.

This book WAS NOT written to teach you how to pray but it's for those that already have a prayer life and just need to know what to say when it pertains to different issues that may occur in your life. For example, issues that don't seem to go away when you just say "the norm," but nothing changes. In this book you will find warfare prayers for most issues that you face as well as scriptures to back it.

You will also find blank pages left for you in order to write down your own prayer request or prayer request for others. You will also find a section in each area of prayers that has been set aside for answered prayers titled, "Testimonial Page." This will allow you to write down your testimonials of when and how God answered your prayers that you presented to Him.

I'm totally excited to release this book and my prayer is that it helps your prayer life to become developed even the more. I also pray that every prayer that you pray, its answer is manifested in your life! GRACE & PEACE!

WHAT IS PRAYER?

Prayer can basically be defined as talking to God but in all actuality it's much more than that. Prayer is an act of worship that glorifies God and reinforces our need for Him. Prayer puts a demand on the promises of God in our lives. Prayer is an act of faith as we believe that what we are summoning God for will manifest.

WHAT IS WARFARE PRAYER?

It is based on the biblical belief of evil/demonic spirits or satanic activity that's known to intervene in human affairs in various ways. Warfare prayers seize all demonic activity that may cause hindrances in prayers being answered. This type of prayer repels these forces and allows for a smoother flow when it pertains to seeing the manifestation of prayers prayed.

Table of Contents

Chapter 1

MANIFESTATIONS OF MIRACLES

SCRIPTURES:

1. Ezekiel 12:28 – Therefore say unto them, Thus saith the Lord God; There shall none of my words be prolonged any more, but the word which I have spoken shall be done, saith the Lord God.

2. Jeremiah 1:12 – Then said the Lord unto me, Thou hast well seen: for I will hasten my word to perform it.

3. Psalm 31:2 – Bow down thine ear to me; deliver me speedily: be thou my strong rock, for an house of defence to save me.

4. Psalm 143:7 – Hear me speedily, O Lord: my spirit faileth: hide not thy face from me, lest I be like unto them that go down into the pit.

5. Psalm 102:2 – Hide not thy face from me in the day when I am in trouble; incline thine ear unto me: in the day when I call answer me speedily.

MANIFESTATION OF MIRACLES
PRAYER POINT: HABAKUK 2:3

- We serve an awesome God! A God that is never late! He comes, He delivers, He makes it happen right on time... right when it needs to happen. He makes all things beautiful in His time. By confessing these powerful words over your life and praying, you will begin to see the manifestations of miracles flow throughout your life.

MANIFESTATION OF MIRACLES
CONFESSION OF PRAISE (SAY THIS ALOUD)

1. I dismiss and disband from my heart and mind every thought, every image, and every picture of failure in the name of Jesus.
2. I reject every spirit of doubt, fear and discouragement in the name of Jesus.
3. I cancel all ungodly delays to the manifestation of my miracles in the name of Jesus.
4. Let the angels of the living God roll away every stone of hindrance in the name of Jesus.
5. O Lord hasten Your word to perform miracles in every area of my life.

MANIFESTATION OF MIRACLES
PRAYER:

Dear God,

I desire breakthroughs concerning (call out the areas you desire to see the manifestation of miracles in your life). I bind every strong man holding my miracle captive. I possess all of my possessions in Jesus name. Everything that God has allotted for (put your name here) will manifest. I break and loose myself from bondage and poverty in the name of Jesus! I release myself from every conscious and unconscious spirit that doesn't align itself with my miracle. Let God arise and let every enemy be scattered. O Lord, please restore all of my wasted years and efforts that I asked you to convert them into blessings, in the name of Jesus. Let the spirit of favor be upon me in the name of Jesus! I lose Your angels in the mighty name of Jesus to go and create favor on my behalf. Father, block every space in my life causing unprofitable leaks in the mighty name of Jesus. I release my miracles from the influence and control of wickedness in Jesus name! O Lord, teach me the divine strategy of prosperity in every area of my life. Lord, quicken my spirit to evolve miracle making ideas. I bind every anti break through, anti miracle and anti prosperity evil force in Jesus name. Let every spirit of blockage be rendered powerless in Jesus name. God, bring sweetness out of bitterness and allow me to find a way where some may say there is no way! God, I thank You now for the manifestation of miracles in my life. I thank You that by Your word and by my faith, it has been released! In the name of Jesus I pray and say this prayer, amen!

Praise and rejoice!

High praise & intensified prayer!

MANIFESTATION OF MIRACLES

Prayer Request For Myself And Others:

1.

2.

3.

4.

5.

6.

7.

8.

9.

10.

11.

12.

13.

14.

15.

16.

17.

18.

19.

20.

MANIFESTATION OF MIRACLES

Testimonial Page:

Linda D. Law

MANIFESTATION OF MIRACLES

Gratitude and Answered Prayers :

Chapter 2

Financial Breakthroughs

SCRIPTURES:

1. Philippians 4:19 – But my God shall supply all your need according to his riches in glory by Christ Jesus.

2. Deuteronomy 8:18 – But thou shalt remember the Lord thy God: for it is he that giveth thee power to get wealth, that he may establish his covenant which he sware unto thy fathers, as it is this day.

3. Psalm 84:11 – For the Lord God is a sun and shield: the Lord will give grace and glory: no good thing will he withhold from them that walk uprightly.

4. Philippians 4:13 – I can do all things through Christ which strengtheneth me.

5. 3 John 1:2 – Beloved, I wish above all things that thou mayest prosper and be in health, even as thy soul prospereth.

FINANCIAL BREAKTHROUGH
PRAYER POINT: (PHIIPPIANS 4:19)

- And my God shall supply all of my needs according to his riches in glory. In order to get the release you want in your finances you must first ask God to give you an immeasurable amount of wisdom to handle what He's allowed you to obtain. After wisdom is implemented you then can expect God to open doors that no one will be able to close! God will supply, you just get in the word and get His wisdom and then watch Him work!

FINANCIAL BREAKTHROUGH
CONFESSION OF PRAISE (SAY THIS ALOUD)

1. I am who God says I am and I possess all possessions that He has deemed mine in Jesus name!
2. I break and loose myself from every curse of financial bondage and poverty in the name of Jesus!
3. May the spirit of favor be upon me everywhere I go concerning my finances in the name of Jesus!
4. Ministering angels bring in prosperity and funds into my finances in Jesus name!
5. Holy Spirit I declare that you are my senior partner in my finances and I get advice and guidance directly from You in Jesus name!

FINANCIAL BREAKTHROUGH PRAYER:

Dear God,

I desire breakthroughs concerning my finances today in the name of Jesus! I refuse to agree with the enemies of my former progress and I cancel any and all ungodly delays in the name of Jesus! Let the angels of the living God cast away every hindrance to the manifestation of my financial breakthroughs! God, let there be turbulence, rearrangement, revision, reorganization and rerouting of situations and circumstances in order to create a path to my desired miracles in the name of Jesus! I bind and render to nothing every anti testimony, anti miracle and anti prosperity force in the name of Jesus. The God who answers by fire and the God of Abraham, Isaac and the God of Jacob is also the God of (insert your name), will answer me by fire in the name of Jesus! This is the same God who answered Moses speedily at the red sea and the God who changed the lot of Jabez. The God who quickens the dead and calls those things that are not as though they were will answer me by fire in the name of Jesus. Let every foreign knee preventing the manifestation of my miracles in my finances in heaven, on earth and under the earth, bow down now over all forces of wickedness in Jesus name. God, I thank you for hearing and answering this prayer... Bring it to pass by fire! In Jesus mighty name! Amen

Praise & rejoice!
High praise & intensified prayer!

FINANCIAL BREAKTHROUGH

Prayer Request For Myself And Others:

1.
2.
3.
4.
5.
6.
7.
8.
9.
10.
11.
12.
13.
14.
15.
16.
17.
18.
19.
20.

Linda D. Law

FINANCIAL BREAKTHROUGH

Testimonial Page:

FINANCIAL BREAKTHROUGH

Gratitude and Answered Prayers :

Chapter 3

New Beginnings

SCRIPTURES:

1. Isaiah 43:19 – Behold, I will do a new thing; now it shall spring forth; shall ye not know it? I will even make a way in the wilderness, and rivers in the desert.

2. 2 Corinthians 5:17 – Therefore if any man be in Christ, he is a new creature: old things are passed away; behold, all things are become new.

3. Ephesians 4:22 – That ye put off concerning the former conversation the old man, which is corrupt according to the deceitful lusts;

4. Isaiah 40:31 – But they that wait upon the Lord shall renew their strength; they shall mount up with wings as eagles; they shall run, and not be weary; and they shall walk, and not faint.

5. 1 Peter 1:3 – Blessed be the God and Father of our Lord Jesus Christ, which according to his abundant mercy hath begotten us again unto a lively hope by the resurrection of Jesus Christ from the dead,

NEW BEGINNINGS
PRAYER POINT: (2 CORINTHIANS 4:16-17)

- Though outwardly we are wasting away yet inwardly we are being renewed day by day. For our light and momentary troubles are achieving for us an eternal glory that far outweighs them all; God will continuously make us new. Every moment of every day brings a fresh and amazing new beginning. God will release you from past hurts and disappointments. You just have to trust and believe that He makes all things new. After these confessions and prayers you will begin to grasp the newness in you...Get ready for new beginnings... Mind, body, soul & spirit!

NEW BEGINNINGS
CONFESSION OF PRAISE (SAY THIS ALOUD)

1. I release myself from the bondage of evil altars and those things that hold me to my past.
2. I cancel every demonic dedication and I break every evil authority over my life now in Jesus name.
3. I apply the blood of Jesus to break all curses in my life and I declare new beginnings.
4. I release myself from the grip of any problem that connects me to my past and I release any negativity that tries to connect to my future.
5. I cancel the consequences of any evil that I may have done that would hinder me from getting to my new beginnings in Jesus name!

NEW BEGINNINGS
PRAYER:

Father God,

I thank you now for who you are and for all You do and for every provision You have made. God, I thank You and I declare that You make all things new in Your timing. I bind the hand of the enemy that would set up entrapments to hold me to my mistakes. I bind the hand of the enemy that would hold me to those I connected to out of pure ignorance. I bind the hand of the enemy that would cause me to struggle financially due to financial ignorance. I thank You now that I am loosed from my past and released from my mistakes. I declare and decree that the devil will no longer hold me hostage and I set fire to his plan, as well as paralyze his operation, in my life in the name of Jesus! I am no longer paying for sins of ignorance; sin that was acted on consciously or unconsciously. I declare that I walk in newness and I am free from the hand of the enemy. I say that his plan concerning me is null and void and will no longer hold me hostage! I am new in Christ and He has granted me a better beginning and I receive it over my life in the name of Jesus!

Praise & rejoice!
High praise & intensified prayer!

NEW BEGINNINGS

Prayer Request For Myself And Others:

1.
2.
3.
4.
5.
6.
7.
8.
9.
10.
11.
12.
13.
14.
15.
16.
17.
18.
19.
20.

Linda D. Law

NEW BEGINNINGS

Testimonial Page:

NEW BEGINNINGS

Gratitude and Answered Prayers :

Chapter 4

Making The Right Decision

SCRIPTURES:

1. Daniel 2:22 – He revealeth the deep and secret things: he knoweth what is in the darkness, and the light dwelleth with him.

2. Ephesians 1:17 – That the God of our Lord Jesus Christ, the Father of glory, may give unto you the spirit of wisdom and revelation in the knowledge of him:

3. Deuteronomy 29:29 – The secret things belong unto the Lord our God: but those things which are revealed belong unto us and to our children for ever, that we may do all the words of this law.

4. Psalm 25:14 – The secret of the Lord is with them that fear him; and he will shew them his covenant.

5. Jeremiah 33:3 – Call unto me, and I will answer thee, and show thee great and mighty things, which thou knowest not.

MAKING THE RIGHT DECISIONS
PRAYER POINTS: (JEREMIAH 33:3)

- To discover the secret things beneficial/detrimental to any particular issue or situation
- To receive revelation knowledge on any issue that you may be experiencing in your life
- To know the mind of God concerning particular issues you may be experiencing in your life

MAKING THE RIGHT DECISIONS
CONFESSION OF PRAISE (SAY THIS ALOUD)

1. O God, to whom no secret is ever hidden, make it known to me whether or not I'm making the right decision.
2. O Lord remove from me any persistent buried grudges, anger against anyone or thing that can possibly block or hinder my spiritual vision.
3. Let every idol present, consciously or unconsciously in my heart concerning this issue be melted away by the fire of the Holy Ghost.
4. O Lord, give unto me the spirit of revelation and wisdom and the knowledge of You, my God.
5. O Lord, reveal to me every secret behind every issue that I face whether beneficial or not! I will make the right decision in every area of my life in Jesus name!

MAKING THE RIGHT DECISIONS
PRAYER:

Dear God,

In the name of Jesus I release myself from every ancestral pol-luted decision maker and I release myself from demonic pollution emanating from my past involvement in religious acts and religion in Jesus name. I break and loose myself from every idol that would hinder me from making Godly decisions. O Lord, teach me to know that which is worth knowing and to love that which is worth loving in the name of Jesus! I refuse to make foundational mistakes in my decision making in the name of Jesus. Guide and direct me in knowing Your mind on particular issues. I stand against any and all satanic attachments that may seek to confuse my decisions. If anything that I choose is not for me, O God, redirect my steps! I bind the activities of unprofitable advice, ungodly impatience, spiritual blindness and deaf, confusing revelations, ungodly pressure and lust in the name of Jesus. Lord, make Your way plain and clear before my eyes, in front of my face and reveal secret things. Open my eyes and help me to make the right decision in Jesus name. Lord God, thank You for the testimo-nies that will follow in Jesus name I pray! Amen!

Praise & rejoice!
High praise & intensified prayer!

MAKING THE RIGHT DECISIONS

Prayer Request For Myself And Others:

1.
2.
3.
4.
5.
6.
7.
8.
9.
10.
11.
12.
13.
14.
15.
16.
17.
18.
19.
20.

Linda D. Law

MAKING THE RIGHT DECISIONS

Testimonial Page:

MAKING THE RIGHT DECISIONS

Gratitude and Answered Prayers :

Chapter 5

Removing Hindrances

SCRIPTURES:

1. Psalm 34:10 –The young lions do lack, and suffer hunger: but they that seek the Lord shall not want any good thing.

2. Psalm 75:6-7 – For promotion cometh neither from the east, nor from the west, nor from the south. But God is the judge: he putteth down one, and setteth up another.

3. Galatians 6:17 – From henceforth let no man trouble me: for I bear in my body the marks of the Lord Jesus.

4. 4.   Psalm 113:5,7-8 – 5 Who is like unto the Lord our God, who dwelleth on high,   7 He raiseth up the poor out of the dust, and lifteth the needy out of the dunghill; 8 That he may set him with princes, even with the princes of his people.

5. Philippians 4:13,19 – 13 I can do all things through Christ which strengtheneth me. 19 But my God shall supply all your need according to his riches in glory by Christ Jesus.

REMOVING HINDRANCES
PRAYER POINTS (PSALM 24:7)

- When you want to excel and be favored in every area of your life
- When you want God to be glorified in your life
- When God gets the glory in your life
- After confessing and praying in this section hindrances will be removed in Jesus name

REMOVING HINDRANCES
CONFESSION OF PRAISE (SAY THIS ALOUD)

1. Thank You Lord because You alone can advance me! Lord, bring me into favor with all those who will decide on my advancement.
2. Lord, cause a divine substitution to happen if this is what will move me ahead according to Your will.
3. I command all evil records, bad reports and word curses be rendered dead in the name of Jesus! Smooth my path and I thank You that it's clear in the name of Jesus.
4. I have the anointing to excel in the name of Jesus and I thank You God for catapulting me into greatness as You did for Daniel in Babylon.
5. God help me to identify and I bless You for helping me to deal with weaknesses that are in me. I declare I am free in Jesus name!

REMOVING HINDRANCES
PRAYER:

Our Father,

We thank You that all gates and doors which constitute hindrances and stumbling blocks in my life cannot withstand the King of Glory and I invite You to intervene in all of my affairs. Lord God, for every red sea there's a Moses; for every wall of Jericho there is a Joshua and for each and every Goliath there is a David. I am a child of God and I'm living according to the word of God. Therefore, whatever hindrances are placed in my path I will overcome and I render them null and void. I silence the hindrances and I deem them powerless in the name of Jesus! I declare that every stumbling block is demolished in Jesus name! O Lord, I dispatch Your angels to roll away every stumbling block that's hindering my advancement and elevation in Jesus name. I receive the mandate to put to flight every enemy concerning my breakthrough in the name of Jesus. To all spirits of strife, demonic opinions, confusion, memory failure, and unprofitable people, I release you from my life in the mighty name of Jesus. Let the mark of the blood of Jesus and divine favor and protection be released upon my life in Jesus name!

Praise & rejoice!
High praise & intensified prayer!

REMOVING HINDRANCES

Prayer Request For Myself And Others:

1.
2.
3.
4.
5.
6.
7.
8.
9.
10.
11.
12.
13.
14.
15.
16.
17.
18.
19.
20.

Linda D. Law

REMOVING HINDRANCES

Testimonial Page:

REMOVING HINDRANCES

Gratitude and Answered Prayers :

Chapter 6

Defeating The Spirit Of Torment

SCRIPTURES:

1. Romans 9:33 - As it is written, Behold, I lay in Sion a stumblingstone and rock of offence: and whosoever believeth on him shall not be ashamed.

2. Romans 16:20 – And the God of peace shall bruise Satan under your feet shortly. The grace of our Lord Jesus Christ be with you. Amen.

3. Ephesians 5:11 – And have no fellowship with the unfruitful works of darkness, but rather reprove them.

4. Numbers 23:23 – Surely there is no enchantment against Jacob, neither is there any divination against Israel: according to this time it shall be said of Jacob and of Israel, What hath God wrought!

5. Isaiah 8:8-10 – 8 And he shall pass through Judah; he shall overflow and go over, he shall reach even to the neck; and the stretching out of his wings shall fill the breadth of thy land, O Immanuel. 9 Associate yourselves, O ye people, and ye shall be broken in pieces; and give ear, all ye of far countries: gird yourselves, and ye shall be broken in pieces; gird yourselves, and ye shall be broken in pieces. 10 Take counsel together, and it shall come to nought; speak the word, and it shall not stand: for God is with us.

DEFEATING THE SPIRIT OF TORMENT
PRAYER POINTS: (ISAIAH 8:9-10)

- When there is evil surrounding and tormenting you
- When you feel as if the whole world is against you
- When the mistakes of your past causes you to regret your present
- After these confessions and prayers you will defeat the spirit of torment in every area of your life

DEFEATING THE SPIRIT OF TORMENT
CONFESSION OF PRAISE (SAY THIS ALOUD)

1. Let every organized strategy of the host of the demonic world against my life be rendered useless in Jesus name.

2. I command all demonic spirits transferred into my life through demonic contacts to be withdrawn and cast into fire in the name of Jesus.

3. Let every demonic influence targeted at destroying my vision, my dream and my kingdom assignment receive total disappointment in Jesus name.

4. I declare and decree that every demonic trap set against my life be shattered to pieces in the name of Jesus.

5. I command all demonic activities against my life to receive disgrace and commotion and all partners in demonic business conspiring against my life to receive commotion and be disorganized in the name of Jesus!

DEFEATING THE SPIRIT OF TORMENT
PRAYER:

Father God in the name of Jesus,

I render the spirit of torment dead in my life. I defeat the spirit of torment by the power of the Holy Ghost and I set fire to every trick plot and plan the enemy and my enemies have derived to make my journey hard! Father God, I declare that the way that I go through obedience and my prayer life is extremely dangerous for the kingdom of darkness, in the name of Jesus. I declare all demonic organized seductive spirits, appearing to pull me down, be rendered null and void in the name of Jesus. Please show me immeasurable forgiveness daily in my life and please don't terminate my spiritual assignments on earth. Yet, help me to accomplish them in the name of Jesus. I ask that You raise Godly intercessors that hear Your voice and obey! These intercessors will always stand privy for me. Lord, let all spiritual gifts and talents in my life begin to operate fully according to Your will and for Your glory, in Jesus name. I reject all uncontrollable crying, heaviness and regrets in the name of Jesus. Please help me in order that my divine spiritual assignments shall not be transferred. I declare that all organized forces of darkness against my life and my spiritual and physical ambition be put to shame, in the name of Jesus. I command this all to be so, in the name of Jesus!

Praise & rejoice!
High praise & intensified prayers!

DEFEATING THE SPIRIT OF TORMENT

Prayer Request For Myself And Others:

1.
2.
3.
4.
5.
6.
7.
8.
9.
10.
11.
12.
13.
14.
15.
16.
17.
18.
19.
20.

Linda D. Law

DEFEATING THE SPIRIT OF TORMENT

Testimonial Page:

DEFEATING THE SPIRIT OF TORMENT

Gratitude and Answered Prayers :

Chapter 7

Multiple Breakthroughs

SCRIPTURES:

1. Psalm 31:2 – Bow down thine ear to me; deliver me speedily: be thou my strong rock, for an house of defence to save me.

2. Isaiah 58:8 – Then shall thy light break forth as the morning, and thine health shall spring forth speedily: and thy righteousness shall go before thee; the glory of the Lord shall be thy reward.

3. Psalm 102:2 – Hide not thy face from me in the day when I am in trouble; incline thine ear unto me: in the day when I call answer me speedily.

4. Jeremiah 1:12 – Then said the Lord unto me, Thou hast well seen: for I will hasten my word to perform it.

5. Jeremiah 29:11 – For I know the thoughts that I think toward you, saith the Lord, thoughts of peace, and not of evil, to give you an expected end.

MULTIPLE BREAKTHROUGHS
PRAYER POINTS: (PSALM 143:7-9)

- When breakthroughs are required in more than one area in your life
- When there is evidence of multiple hindrances to your breakthroughs
- When you are experiencing "no doors open" syndrome in your life
- After confessing and praying in this section you will experience multiple breakthroughs in your life

MULTIPLE BREAKTHROUGHS
CONFESSION OF PRAISE (SAY THIS ALOUD)

1. All boasting demons in human form delegated against me will be silenced.
2. I withdraw my benefits from the hand of the oppressors and I declare that all unprofitable marks in my life be erased with the blood of Jesus.
3. Let every power chasing away my blessings be paralyzed. Let everything that's good for my life and being eaten up by the enemy, be released in the name of Jesus.
4. Let heavenly fire ignite my prayer life and I declare and decree it to be so, in the name of Jesus.
5. Let the anointing for spiritual breakthroughs fall mightily on me, in the name of Jesus.

MULTIPLE BREAKTHROUGHS PRAYERS:

Father God in the name of Jesus,

Let the anointing for spiritual breakthroughs fall mightily on me, in the name of Jesus. Lord, empower my prayer life and cause me to be a prayer addict that receives multiple breakthroughs throughout my life. I revive and ignite my prayer life by the power of the Holy Ghost. I render every negative plan and activity against my life to be reversed to good. I declare the touch of Your anointing and Your power will fall upon me now. Lord, give me divine prescriptions to my problems today and give me power to overcome obstacles to obtain breakthroughs. I declare that the word of God will explode in me and all spiritual holes leaking blessings will be closed in Jesus name. I declare I will retain all blessings that are afforded me by the power of the Holy Ghost. My Lord God will assist me in locating any and every defect in the clay of my life. I bind the spirit of negative destiny in every area of my life in the name of Jesus. Lord, please allow me to be at the right place at the right time to receive miracles, manifestations and multiple breakthroughs in Jesus name!

Praise & rejoice!
High praise & intensifies prayer!

MULTIPLE BREAKTHROUGHS

Prayer Request For Myself And Others:

1.
2.
3.
4.
5.
6.
7.
8.
9.
10.
11.
12.
13.
14.
15.
16.
17.
18.
19.
20.

Linda D. Law

MULTIPLE BREAKTHROUGHS

Testimonial Page:

MULTIPLE BREAKTHROUGHS

Gratitude and Answered Prayers :

Chapter 8

Hard Situations

SCRIPTURES:

1. Job 5:12 – He disappointeth the devices of the crafty, so that their hands cannot perform their enterprise.

2. Isaiah 54:17 – No weapon that is formed against thee shall prosper; and every tongue that shall rise against thee in judgment thou shalt condemn. This is the heritage of the servants of the Lord, and their righteousness is of me, saith the Lord.

3. Jeremiah 1:8,19 – 8 Be not afraid of their faces: for I am with thee to deliver thee, saith the Lord. 19 And they shall fight against thee; but they shall not prevail against thee; for I am with thee, saith the Lord, to deliver thee.

4. Deuteronomy 33:25-27 – 25 Thy shoes shall be iron and brass; and as thy days, so shall thy strength be. 26 There is none like unto the God of Jeshurun, who rideth upon the heaven in thy help, and in his excellency on the sky. 27 The eternal God is thy refuge, and underneath are the everlasting arms: and he shall thrust out the enemy from before thee; and shall say, Destroy them.

5. Romans 16:20 – And the God of peace shall bruise Satan under your feet shortly. The grace of our Lord Jesus Christ be with you. Amen.

HARD SITUATIONS
PRAYER POINTS: (PSALM 18)

- When everything you attempt to do is simply hard to do
- To defeat hard situations and stubborn forces in your life
- When it seems you've tried everything and nothing works for you
- After these confessions and prayers and with applying your faith God will cause your hard situations to turn for your favor and work for your good

HARD SITUATIONS
CONFESSION OF PRAISE (SAY THIS ALOUD)

1.   Praise and worship the most high for He reigns! Let God arise in His anger and fight for me.
2.   I refuse to allow my angels of blessings to depart and I cancel every evil effect of names from evil origins in my life.
3.   I paralyze all aggression addressed to me and I declare all problems neutralized that originated from the mistakes of my parents in the name of Jesus.
4.   I declare that you will bring sweetness and every good thing out of bitterness for me and all the food doors of my life that holds wickedness be shut.
5.   I speak with authority that all anti breakthroughs designed against my life be shattered to pieces in the name of Jesus.

HARD SITUATIONS
PRAYER:

God my Father,

I command my destiny to begin to change in the name of Jesus. Let my hand become the sword of fire to cut down demonic trees from the root and allow my hand to become the sword of fire to manifest this! Let the stomping of my feet defeat the camp of the enemy of all boastful evil powers that have been delegated against me, be silenced, in Jesus name. I withdraw my benefits from the hand of the oppressors and I declare all powers chasing blessings away, with their negative words and impure thoughts, be paralyzed in the name of Jesus. Let the enemy begin to vomit every good thing that he has eaten up in my life in the name of Jesus. Lord, give me power to overcome every hard situation. I clear my goods from the warehouse of the strong man and in the name of Jesus all hidden arrows be troubled in their secret hiding places. I frustrate and disappoint every instrument of the enemy fashioned against me and I disarm every enemy who troubles my present or my future to be rendered powerless. I take authority over every satanic attack on my home and I withdraw the staff of office of the strongman delegated against me, in the name of Jesus. I stand against every faith destroyer and every unprofitable agreement and reconciliation in Jesus name. I declare that every hard situation is burned by the fire of the Holy Ghost in Jesus name!

Praise & rejoice!
High praise & intensified prayer!

HARD SITUATUATIONS

Prayer Request For Myself And Others:

1.
2.
3.
4.
5.
6.
7.
8.
9.
10.
11.
12.
13.
14.
15.
16.
17.
18.
19.
20.

Linda D. Law

HARD SITUATIONS

Testimonial Page:

HARD SITUATIONS

Gratitude and Answered Prayers :

Chapter 9

Growing Spiritually

SCRIPTURES:

1. Philippians 3:10,14 – [10] That I may know him, and the power of his resurrection, and the fellowship of his sufferings, being made conformable unto his death;[14] I press toward the mark for the prize of the high calling of God in Christ Jesus.

2. Hebrews 5:12 – For when for the time ye ought to be teachers, ye have need that one teach you again which be the first principles of the oracles of God; and are become such as have need of milk, and not of strong meat.

3. Colossians 2:7 – Rooted and built up in him, and stablished in the faith, as ye have been taught, abounding therein with thanksgiving.

4. John 3: 29-30 – [29] He that hath the bride is the bridegroom: but the friend of the bridegroom, which standeth and heareth him, rejoiceth greatly because of the bridegroom's voice: this my joy therefore is fulfilled. [30] He must increase, but I must decrease.

5. Hebrews 6:1 – Therefore leaving the principles of the doctrine of Christ, let us go on unto perfection; not laying again the foundation of repentance from dead works, and of faith toward God,

GROWING SPIRITUALLY
PRAYER POINTS: (JOHN 3:30)

- For those who desire meaningful spiritual growth in their walk with God
- For those that feel as if you cannot attain a certain level in the spirit
- For those who need to humble themselves in order that God will elevate them
- After you finish this section and you've applied your faith, over time God will mature you spiritually

GROWING SPIRITUALLY
CONFESSION OF PRAISE (SAY THIS ALOUD)

1. I am comforted in my heart! I declare that I'm established in every good word that God has placed over my life.
2. I am filled with the knowledge of Gods will and I have all wisdom and spiritual understanding.
3. God I declare that You will assist me in walking worthy of Your wisdom, Your knowledge, Your understanding and Your discernment in Jesus name.
4. I am open to my knowledge of God being increased by way of the Holy Spirit.
5. Father God, allow my mind, body, soul and spirit to be counted worthy and blameless until the coming of our Lord and Savior Jesus Christ! I receive growth and I will not be deterred from any good thing in my life.

GROWING SPIRITUALLY
PRAYER:

O Lord,

Increase me in the knowledge of You and strengthen me mightily. Father God, I declare that I'm filled with wisdom and my eyes of understanding are enlightened in the name of Jesus. Let me be strengthened with might by His spirit in my inner man and I declare that Christ dwells in my heart by faith. Father, allow me to be rooted and grounded in patience, love and understanding and allow me to be filled with God's goodness and power. God help me comprehend the breadth, length, depth and height of the love and grace and mercy of Christ Jesus. Let the word of the Lord have free course and be glorified within me and the Lord of peace grants me peace in every area of my life, in Jesus name. I declare the utterance be given unto me to make known the mystery of the gospel and I am being made perfect unto Your good work. Let the grace of the Lord Jesus Christ be with me and injected with Your goodness, that will cause me to be spiritually healthy and will boost my appetite for Your word. God, infuse into my bloodline the blood of Your Son, Jesus, that will produce an absolute hunger and thirst for Your will and Your way, throughout the entirety of my life in Jesus name. Thank You God for Your everlasting joy and peace. I bless You for new spiritual heights and I believe by faith I am lifted in the mighty name of Jesus! Amen!

Praise & rejoice!
High praise & intensified prayer!

GROWING SPIRITUALLY

Prayer Request For Myself And Others:

1.
2.
3.
4.
5.
6.
7.
8.
9.
10.
11.
12.
13.
14.
15.
16.
17.
18.
19.
20.

Linda D. Law

GROWING SPIRITUALLY

Testimonial Page:

GROWING SPIRITUALLY

Gratitude and Answered Prayers :

Chapter 10

Barrenness & Unfruitfulness

SCRIPTURES:

1. Romans 4:19 – And being not weak in faith, he considered not his own body now dead, when he was about an hundred years old, neither yet the deadness of Sarah's womb:

2. Galatians 3:13-14 – [13] Christ hath redeemed us from the curse of the law, being made a curse for us: for it is written, Cursed is every one that hangeth on a tree: [14] That the blessing of Abraham might come on the Gentiles through Jesus Christ; that we might receive the promise of the Spirit through faith.

3. Mathew 8:17 – That it might be fulfilled which was spoken by Esaias the prophet, saying, Himself took our infirmities, and bare our sicknesses.

4. Matthew 3:10 – And now also the axe is laid unto the root of the trees: therefore every tree which bringeth not forth good fruit is hewn down, and cast into the fire.

5. Isaiah 58:8 – Then shall thy light break forth as the morning, and thine health shall spring forth speedily: and thy righteousness shall go before thee; the glory of the Lord shall be thy reward.

BARREN/UNFRUITFUL
PRAYER POINTS: (LUKE 10:19)

- For those who may have been told that it is medically impossible to have children
- For those who seek God's face concerning the fruit of their womb
- For those who are experiencing barrenness or unfruitfulness in any area of your life
- After you've confessed and prayed, God will supernaturally grant your request. Have faith and believe!

BARREN/UNFRUITFUL
CONFESSION OF PRAISE (SAY THIS ALOUD)

1. God, I thank You for Your power to deliver me from any form of bondage.
2. I now ask for forgiveness for myself and the sins of my ancestors that are known and unknown. I declare the blood of Jesus separates me from the sins of my ancestors.
3. I denounce any evil dedication placed upon my life and I declare I am loosed from every negative word placed upon my life.
4. Lord, I declare that I am separated from all sins of my forefathers by the precious blood of Jesus.
5. I declare and decree that the curse of barrenness and unfruitfulness are broken off of my life right now in Jesus name.

BARREN/UNFRUITFULNESS
PRAYER:

O Lord,

Hasten Your word to perform in every area of my life. I ask that You revenge me speedily from the hands of my adversaries. I refuse to agree with the enemies of my progress and I declare the fire of God saturate my womb and spirit in the name of Jesus. Let every design conjured up to destroy my life and future be rendered completely and nullified. I pray all evil labels, fashioned by the camp of the enemy against my life, be silenced by the blood of Jesus. I release every satanic deposit made against my life in the mighty name of Jesus. I break myself loose from the bondage of stagnancy. Allow the blood, fire and living water of our most high God wash my system clean from every unprofitable growth in my womb. I bind all impurities and evil consumptions, secret sicknesses and all unprofitable deposits, made knowingly and unknowingly to hinder my supply, in the name of Jesus. I reject all evil manipulation and manipulators and I break the grip of witchcraft and familiar spirits over my life in the name of Jesus. I reject any and all satanic deposits of barrenness in my intestines, in the name of Jesus. I reject any deposits made against my womb or any other organ in my body. I declare that I am fruitful and will multiply in the areas of my life that have been barren according to God's will. I declare that every area of my life is too hot for any evil entity to inhabit. I command all evil growth in my life be uprooted in Jesus name. I declare this to be so! I declare it all in the name of Jesus!

Praise & rejoice!
High praise & intensified prayers!

BARREN/UNFRUITFULNESS

Prayer Request For Myself And Others:

1.
2.
3.
4.
5.
6.
7.
8.
9.
10.
11.
12.
13.
14.
15.
16.
17.
18.
19.
20.

Linda D. Law

BARREN/UNFRUITFULNESS

Testimonial Page:

BARREN/UNFRUITFULNESS

Gratitude and Answered Prayers :

Chapter 11

Household Opposition

SCRIPTURES:

1. Matthew 10:36 – And a man's foes shall be they of his own household.

2. Genesis 50:20 – But as for you, ye thought evil against me; but God meant it unto good, to bring to pass, as it is this day, to save much people alive.

3. Micah 7:6-7 – [6]For the son dishonoureth the father, the daughter riseth up against her mother, the daughter in law against her mother in law; a man's enemies are the men of his own house. [7] Therefore I will look unto the Lord; I will wait for the God of my salvation: my God will hear me.

4. Obadiah 1:3-4 – [3] The pride of thine heart hath deceived thee, thou that dwellest in the clefts of the rock, whose habitation is high; that saith in his heart, Who shall bring me down to the ground? [4]Though thou exalt thyself as the eagle, and though thou set thy nest among the stars, thence will I bring thee down, saith the Lord.

5. Colossians 3:13 – Forbearing one another, and forgiving one another, if any man have a quarrel against any: even as Christ forgave you, so also do ye.

HOUSEHOLD OPPOSITION/WICKEDNESS
PRAYER POINTS (GENESIS 50:20)

- When your strongest opposition is within your own household
- When there is opposition against you by people you know; family
- When household wickedness, such as witchcraft, hinders you in your day to day life
- In this section we will attack and conquer household opposition and wickedness

HOUSEHOLD OPPOSITION/WICKEDNESS
CONFESSION OF PRAISE (SAY THIS ALOUD)

1. Lord, allow every evil imagination against me to wither away from the root and those that would laugh at me to scorn and witness Gods testimony concerning my life.
2. Lord, allow the destructive plan of my enemies that are aimed against me to blow up in their faces. Let the cause of my ridicule be converted to a source of miracle. I declare it to be so.
3. Lord, allow all powers sponsoring evil decisions against me to be disregarded and let the stubborn strong man appointed against me fall down to the ground and be rendered powerless, in the name of Jesus.
4. Lord, allow every spirit of Balaam sent to curse me fall after the order of Balaam.
5. Lord, allow all satanic manipulations aimed at changing my destiny to be confused, frustrated and annihilated in the powerful name of Jesus. I declare household evil and opposition is rendered dead in the name of Jesus.

HOUSEHOLD OPPOSITION/WICKEDNESS PRAYER:

Father God in the name of Jesus,

I command that every blessing to be snatched by witchcraft and word curses be released now, in the name of Jesus. I command every blessing snatched by familiar spirits, ancestral spirits, envious friends, and envious enemies, and satanic agents, rulers of darkness, evil powers, and spiritual wickedness in heavenly places, to be released by the power of the Holy Ghost. Lord, allow all the weapons of my oppressors and tormentors to be rendered powerless in the name of Jesus. Let the fire of God destroy all powers working against me. Let all evil advice given against my favor crash and disintegrate. Let every tree planted by fear in my life rise up from the roots. I cancel all curses spoken by those in my household to be rendered dead in the name of Jesus. I cut myself off from every territorial spirit, witchcraft and bewitchment curse in the name of Jesus. I cancel the power of curses upon my life. I bind the strong man over my life, the life of my family, and over my blessings over my business/job. I command the strongman to be burned by the fire of the Holy Ghost, in the name of Jesus. I command all curses issued against me within and without my household, to be cancelled by the blood of Jesus and the power of the Holy Ghost, in the mighty name of Jesus. I declare it to be so.

Praise & rejoice!
High praise & intensified prayer!

HOUSEHOLD OPPOSITION/WICKEDNESS

Prayer Request For Myself And Others:

1.
2.
3.
4.
5.
6.
7.
8.
9.
10.
11.
12.
13.
14.
15.
16.
17.
18.
19.
20.

Linda D. Law

HOUSEHOLD OPPOSITION/WICKEDNESS

Testimonial Page:

HOUSEHOLD OPPOSITION/WICKEDNESS

Gratitude and Answered Prayers :

Chapter 12

Marital Issues

SCRIPTURES:

1. Matthew 19:6 – Wherefore they are no more twain, but one flesh. What therefore God hath joined together, let not man put asunder.

2. Jeremiah 1:10 – See, I have this day set thee over the nations and over the kingdoms, to root out, and to pull down, and to destroy, and to throw down, to build, and to plant.

3. Genesis 1:26 – And God said, Let us make man in our image, after our likeness: and let them have dominion over the fish of the sea, and over the fowl of the air, and over the cattle, and over all the earth, and over every creeping thing that creepeth upon the earth.

4. Genesis 3:15 – And I will put enmity between thee and the woman, and between thy seed and her seed; it shall bruise thy head, and thou shalt bruise his heel.

5. Ephesians 5:31 – For this cause shall a man leave his father and mother, and shall be joined unto his wife, and they two shall be one flesh.

MARITAL ISSUES
PRAYER POINTS: (JOB 11:4-20)

- To stop the activities of Satan as he invades, disrupts and attempts to destroy your marriage
- To pray against adultery in your marriage
- When the fire in your marriage is no longer there and you desire that God restore and replenish it
- With prayer, you will pray your way back to what God intended your marriage to be initially
- If you haven't been giving 110%, you must vow to do so in every area

MARITAL ISSUES
CONFESSION OF PRAISE (SAY THIS ALOUD)

1. God, I thank You for intervening in my marriage in the name of Jesus.
2. I render anything and everything to be destroyed that will attempt to stand between my marriage and this prayer confession.
3. I declare that the anointing to pray to the point of my breakthrough in my marriage is flowing upon me now.
4. Lord Jesus, I invite You to come to my aid in every difficult situation in my marriage now.
5. I declare and decree, in the name of Jesus, that any demonic marital intrusion and division will stand powerless in my marriage.

MARITAL ISSUES
PRAYER:

Father God,

In the name of Jesus I declare that my union, my marriage to (say his/her name) is divinely connected by You. I declare and decree that what You've joined together, no man will put asunder. Right now I deposit peace, harmony love, unity and continuance between us. Let any strange and unholy affair be rendered null and void by the fire of the Holy Ghost. Lord, I bind all evil arrows fired from strange individuals presently in my marriage, that You have ordained, lose their grip upon my marriage and return to your sender. Angel of God, go right away and disconnect the relationship between my husband/wife and any strange individual in the mighty name of Jesus. I nullify every evil judgment against me and my marriage. Let all hindrances, to the manifestations of my restoration; depart from us now in the name of Jesus. God of new beginnings, please begin a new thing in my marriage. May the blood of the lamb flow into the foundation of my marriage and give it a fresh release of life. I declare that anything causing disturbance in my marriage be dismantled by the fire of the Holy Ghost. Father God, I thank You that I submit to the authority of the Holy Ghost and I bless you for restoring the joy of my marriage in the mighty name of Jesus.

Praise & rejoice!
High praise & intensified prayer!

MARITAL ISSUSES

Prayer Request For Myself And Others:

1.
2.
3.
4.
5.
6.
7.
8.
9.
10.
11.
12.
13.
14.
15.
16.
17.
18.
19.
20.

Linda D. Law

MARITAL ISSUSES

Testimonial Page:

MARITAL ISSUSES

Gratitude and Answered Prayers :

Chapter 13

Hedge Of Protection

SCRIPTURES:

1. Psalm 34:7 – The angel of the Lord encampeth round about them that fear him, and delivereth them.

2. James 4:7 – Submit yourselves therefore to God. Resist the devil, and he will flee from you.

3. Job 1:10 – Hast not thou made an hedge about him, and about his house, and about all that he hath on every side? Thou hast blessed the work of his hands, and his substance is increased in the land.

4. John 14:6 – Jesus saith unto him, I am the way, the truth, and the life: no man cometh unto the Father, but by me.

5. Psalm 91:1 – He that dwelleth in the secret place of the most High shall abide under the shadow of the Almighty.

HEDGE OF PROTECTION
PRAYER POINTS: (LUKE 15:14-16)

- When you need Gods protection more so than ever before
- When you need Gods protection from hurt harm and danger that seems to be constant in your life
- When you're being manipulated in certain areas of your life and you need Gods divine protection
- God will cover you... God will protect you... God has you covered

HEDGE OF PROTECTION
CONFESSION OF PRAISE (SAY THIS ALOUD)

1. I bind every evil force that will attempt to come against my life that causes harm against me.
2. I denounce every evil threat that has been spoken against me by my enemy.
3. I confess that I am protected and I am covered by the blood of Jesus.
4. I render every evil word and curse spoken over my life falls to the ground and die. I render word curses powerless.
5. I declare and decree that I am hidden in the secret place of the almighty. I declare a hedge of protection covers me continuously.

HEDGE OF PROTECTION
PRAYER:

Father God in the name of Jesus,

I pray now for Your protection, power, and covering in the name of Jesus. I command angels of protection to surround me in Jesus name. I command angels that are sitting dormant and waiting to be assigned to go now and war in the realm of the spirit. Lord, may they bring those things to past concerning me, that the enemy has attempted to hinder. I command the fire of the Holy Ghost burn every evil word and evil deed done to destroy my destiny. I dismantle every evil operating force that is set as traps to deter me from my destined placed in the kingdom. I call out every manipulator and the very spirit of manipulation. I render it dead in Jesus name. I command now that every trick and plot, every plan that's spoken against my future is counted as null and void. I declare that I am the righteousness of God. I am obedient to His commands and because of this if I declare and decree anything, according to His will, He will establish it on the earth. I declare that a hedge of protection is around my mind, emotions and health! I declare it to be so, in Jesus name and in His name I pray... Amen.

Praise & rejoice!
High praise & intensified prayer!

HEDGE OF PROTECTION

Prayer Request For Myself And Others:

1.
2.
3.
4.
5.
6.
7.
8.
9.
10.
11.
12.
13.
14.
15.
16.
17.
18.
19.
20.

Linda D. Law

HEDGE OF PROTECTION

Testimonial Page:

HEDGE OF PROTECTION

Gratitude and Answered Prayers :

Chapter 14

Court Intervention

SCRIPTURES:

1. Proverbs 21:1 – The king's heart is in the hand of the Lord, as the rivers of water: he turneth it whithersoever he will.

2. Psalm 62:11 – God hath spoken once; twice have I heard this; that power belongeth unto God.

3. Proverbs 16:1 – The preparations of the heart in man, and the answer of the tongue, is from the Lord.

4. Jeremiah 1:9 – And they shall fight against thee; but they shall not prevail against thee; for I am with thee, saith the Lord, to deliver thee.

5. Nahum 1: 7-8 – [7] The Lord is good, a strong hold in the day of trouble; and he knoweth them that trust in him. [8] But with an overrunning flood he will make an utter end of the place thereof, and darkness shall pursue his enemies.

COURT INTERVENTION (CONSPIRACY AGAINST YOU)
PRAYER POINTS: (ISAIAH 54:15)

- When you need a court case decided in your favor because you are innocent
- When you simply have a court case
- When you're facing a panel which decides your fate and you need Gods favor

COURT INTERVENTION (CONSPIRACY AGAINST YOU)
CONFESSION OF PRAISE (SAY THIS ALOUD)

1. God, I thank You and I claim victory over every adversary in this court case in Jesus name.
2. I bind and paralyze the strongman employed or delegated to disgrace me in Jesus name.
3. Let all the affairs of my life be too hot for any evil power to manipulate.
4. Grant my lawyer and me supernatural wisdom to subdue all opposition.
5. Lord let it be impossible for my adversary to subdue the truth in this matter.

COURT INTERVENTION (CONSPIRACY AGAINST YOU) PRAYER:

The Lord is with me as a mighty terrible one. Therefore, my persecutors shall stumble and not prevail in my life. They shall be put to shame and confusion shall be theirs, concerning me, in the name of Jesus. I close every negative door that the enemy may want to open, using this case or any case against me. I command you satanic agents to clear out the pathway to my victory, in the name of Jesus. I cancel any demonic decision and expectation concerning this case. Father, please make it possible for me to obtain favor in the sight of the judge, in the name of Jesus. Lord, I declare and decree that I will find favor, compassion and loving kindness with each juror assigned. I declare that all demonic obstacles, that have been established in the heart of anyone against my prosperity, be destroyed in the mighty name of Jesus. Lord, allow the fire of the Holy Spirit to purge my life from any evil mark put upon my name and confuse the tongues of those that are possibly gathered to do me harm, in the name of Jesus. I declare and decree that those that have or will conspire against my assignments will be rendered dead, void and nullified in the name of Jesus. I command angels that excel in strength to hearken unto the voice of the word of the Lord thy God. May they go now and war in the realm of the spirit, bringing me victory in the name of Jesus. Amen.

Praise & rejoice!
High praise & intensified prayer!

COURT INTERVENTION

Prayer Request For Myself And Others:

1.
2.
3.
4.
5.
6.
7.
8.
9.
10.
11.
12.
13.
14.
15.
16.
17.
18.
19.
20.

Linda D. Law

COURT INTERVENTION

Testimonial Page:

COURT INTERVENTION

Gratitude and Answered Prayers :

Chapter 15

Binding The Strongman

SCRIPTURES:

1. Matthew 12:29 – Or else how can one enter into a strong man's house, and spoil his goods, except he first bind the strong man? And then he will spoil his house.

2. Mark 3:27 – No man can enter into a strong man's house, and spoil his goods, except he will first bind the strong man; and then he will spoil his house.

3. Luke 11:21 – When a strong man armed keepeth his palace, his goods are in peace:

4. Psalm 24:7-10 – 7 Lift up your heads, O ye gates; and be ye lift up, ye everlasting doors; and the King of glory shall come in. 8 Who is this King of glory? The Lord strong and mighty, the Lord mighty in battle. 9 Lift up your heads, O ye gates; even lift them up, ye everlasting doors; and the King of glory shall come in. 10 Who is this King of glory? The Lord of hosts, he is the King of glory. Selah.

5. Isaiah 49:25 – But thus saith the Lord, Even the captives of the mighty shall be taken away, and the prey of the terrible shall be delivered: for I will contend with him that contendeth with thee, and I will save thy children.

BINDING THE STRONGMAN
PRAYER POINTS: (DUETERONOMY 33:27)

- When you desire to unseat the strongman on your job, your business and your career
- When you desire to unseat the strongman in your home and within your family
- When you desire to unseat the strongman in your faith and in your finances

*strongman (definition) – a leader who rules by the exercise of threats, force or violence.

BINDING THE STRONGMAN
CONFESSION OF PRAISE (SAY THIS ALOUD)

1. God, I thank You that the gates of hell shall not prevail against me.
2. I bind the strongman assigned against my life and I declare that I am free in every area of my life.
3. I declare that the wisdom of all evil counselors, including the strongman, be rendered with a value of nothing.
4. Let the strongman pursuing me be rendered powerless and I declare it to be so.
5. I unseat every stronghold delegated against me.
6. I declare that I'm loosed from all strongholds in Jesus name.

BINDING THE STRONGMAN
PRAYER:

O God,

I command all the dark work, being done against my life in secret, to be exposed and be nullified in the name of Jesus. O' Lord, if my life is on the wrong course, please correct me in order that any evil plot or plan will be rendered of no effect in my life. Let every anti progress altar that is fashioned against me be destroyed by the fire of the Holy Ghost. I command my destiny for change to be better than ever because the strongman has been commanded to lose his grip over my life, mind, money, family, children, job, business, ideas, health, peace and any thing that concerns me or my destiny in the name of Jesus. Allow my hands to become a sword of fire so they may cut down demonic trees from the root. I command all boastful powers delegated against me to be silenced permanently in the name of Jesus. I disable and disband any wicked gatherings held in the spirit realm against me. Lord, allow my office, car, home and any and all of my properties to be too hot for the strongman to handle in the name of Jesus. Lord, let the evil strongman delegated against me be silenced. In the name of Jesus I declare that I am free and full of power in Jesus name.

Rejoice & praise!
High praise & intensified prayers!

BINDING THE STRONGMAN

Prayer Request For Myself And Others:

1.
2.
3.
4.
5.
6.
7.
8.
9.
10.
11.
12.
13.
14.
15.
16.
17.
18.
19.
20.

Linda D. Law

BINDING THE STRONGMAN

Testimonial Page:

BINDING THE STRONGMAN

Gratitude and Answered Prayers :

Chapter 16

Godly Spouses For Our Children

SCRIPTURES:

1. Matthew 7:7 – Ask, and it shall be given you; seek, and ye shall find; knock, and it shall be opened unto you:

2. Joshua 24:15 – And if it seem evil unto you to serve the Lord, choose you this day whom ye will serve; whether the gods which your fathers served that were on the other side of the flood, or the gods of the Amorites, in whose land ye dwell: but as for me and my house, we will serve the Lord.

3. Isaiah 54:17 – No weapon that is formed against thee shall prosper; and every tongue that shall rise against thee in judgment thou shalt condemn. This is the heritage of the servants of the Lord, and their righteousness is of me, saith the Lord.

4. Isaiah 54:13 – And all thy children shall be taught of the Lord; and great shall be the peace of thy children.

5. Isaiah 49:25 – But thus saith the Lord, Even the captives of the mighty shall be taken away, and the prey of the terrible shall be delivered: for I will contend with him that contendeth with thee, and I will save thy children.

GODLY SPOUSES FOR OUR CHILDREN
PRAYER POINTS: (GENESIS 24:3-4)

- Prayers designed for parents who want their children to be in covenant with Godly husbands/wives
- A concerned parent like Abraham would not undermine the importance of seeking the face of the Lord to know the God chosen life partner for his son.
- The person your child marries will determine his/her eternal destiny
- We believe God for our children
- With faith and confessions, along with prayers, this will happen

GODLY SPOUSES FOR OUR CHILDREN
CONFESSION OF PRAISE (SAY THIS ALOUD)

1. God, I thank You, because You alone knows who's best for my son/daughter.
2. Lord, I thank You for releasing the man/woman you have predestined as my son/daughter's covenant partner.
3. Lord, I thank You that this divine connection will come at the appointed time according to Your will.
4. Lord, I thank You that the person you have pre-ordained from the foundation of this world loves You wholeheartedly.
5. God, I bless You, that their home will be established according to scripture.

GODLY SPOUSES FOR OUR CHILDREN
PRAYER:

Father God in the name of Jesus,

I declare that any and all satanic barriers, keeping or that will keep my son/daughter from connection, be dissolved in the name of Jesus. Lord, I ask that You send forth Your warring angels to battle on their behalf. Lord God, I believe You have created my daughter/son for a special kind, God loving, worshipping man/woman of God. I command Your hand to move concerning them in the precious name of Jesus. I stand in the gap and call him/her out by obscurity into direct alignment with his/her life in the name of Jesus. I reject the provision of counterfeit spouses, who the enemy sent, to deter destiny or cause time to be wasted in the life of my son/daughter in Jesus name. I cut off the flow of any inherited marital problems into the life of my child(ren) and I declare that patience, love, joy, and peace will reign in the life of my son/daughter until the right person comes along. I pray this prayer in the matchless name of Jesus. Father in the name of Jesus, just as Abraham sent his servant to find his son Isaac a wife, please send the Holy Spirit to bring my son/daughter future wife/husband to him/her. I thank You Lord, for the answer in Jesus name.

Praise & rejoice
High praise & intensified prayer!

GODLY SPOUSES FOR OUR CHILDREN

Prayer Request For Myself And Others:

1.
2.
3.
4.
5.
6.
7.
8.
9.
10.
11.
12.
13.
14.
15.
16.
17.
18.
19.
20.

Linda D. Law

GODLY SPOUSES FOR OUR CHILDREN

Testimonial Page:

GODLY SPOUSES FOR OUR CHILDREN

Gratitude and Answered Prayers :

Chapter 17

Restoration

SCRIPTURES:

1. Job 42:10 – And the Lord turned the captivity of Job, when he prayed for his friends: also the Lord gave Job twice as much as he had before.

2. John 10:10 – Jesus said: I am come that they might have life, and that they might have it more abundantly.

3. Joel 2:25-26 – [25] And I will restore to you the years that the locust hath eaten, the cankerworm, and the caterpiller, and the palmerworm, my great army which I sent among you. [26] And ye shall eat in plenty, and be satisfied, and praise the name of the Lord your God, that hath dealt wondrously with you: and my people shall never be ashamed.

4. Isaiah 41:18-20 – [18] I will open rivers in high places, and fountains in the midst of the valleys: I will make the wilderness a pool of water, and the dry land springs of water. [19] I will plant in the wilderness the cedar, the shittah tree, and the myrtle, and the oil tree; I will set in the desert the fir tree, and the pine, and the box tree together: [20] That they may see, and know, and consider, and understand together, that the hand of the Lord hath done this, and the Holy One of Israel hath created it.

5. Romans 8:28 – And we know that all things work together for good to them that love God, to them who are the called according to his purpose.

RESTORATION
PRAYER POINT (ZECHARIAH 10:6)

- Example: When you lose your job in an unrighteous way or when something that you treasure has been stolen. When you want to possess your possessions and you desire recovery.

No matter the spiritual height from which you have fallen, God is very much interested in restoring you if you can cry unto Him for mercy. As you confess and pray, the power of restoration will be released in your life.

RESTORATION
CONFESSION OF PRAISE (SAY THIS ALOUD)

1. God, I thank You for Your precious son Jesus.
2. Lord, thank you for opening doors of opportunity to me through this prayer.
3. I declare all evil and unknown forces set up against my life be scattered.
4. I confess my part in this because of immaturity and a lack of wisdom. However, I claim the victory in every area of my life.
5. I recover any and everything that is deemed beneficial in my life. I speak restoration even now over every area of my life.

RESTORATION
PRAYER:

Father God in the name of Jesus,

Right now I recover all ground that it seems I may have lost to the enemy. I bind the spirit of depression and frustration in my life in the name of Jesus. Heavenly angels, perform the necessary procedures in every area of my life. Lord Jesus, carry out all the repairs that are necessary in my life in Jesus name. I command all the damages done to my life by evil words spoken, personal negative confessions and household wickedness to be nullified in the name of Jesus. Lord, allow all parasites feeding on my life, in any area, be rendered dead. Fire of God; consume the clock of the enemy that is working against my life. I declare that my life is not a fertile ground for any evil to thrive in. I claim this in the name of Jesus. I command all doors of good and perfect things that were closed against me by the enemy to be reopened... Great and effectual doors open now, in the name of Jesus. I reject the spirit of impossibility and I claim doors restored and reopened. I declare restoration 100 fold in every area of my life. I declare my life to be one miracle after the other, in the name of Jesus. I possess the power to pursue, possess, overtake and recover my goods from the hand of the enemy. I declare that I am restored, rejuvenated and empowered by the blood of Jesus. I declare this all to be so in Jesus name.

Praise & rejoice!
High praise & intensified prayer!

RESTORATION

Prayer Request For Myself And Others:

1.
2.
3.
4.
5.
6.
7.
8.
9.
10.
11.
12.
13.
14.
15.
16.
17.
18.
19.
20.

Linda D. Law

RESTORATION

Testimonial Page:

RESTORATION

Gratitude and Answered Prayers :

Chapter 18

Employment

1. Deuteronomy 28:13 – And the Lord shall make thee the head, and not the tail; and thou shalt be above only, and thou shalt not be beneath; if that thou hearken unto the commandments of the Lord thy God, which I command thee this day, to observe and to do them:

2. Proverbs 21:1 - The king's heart is in the hand of the Lord, as the rivers of water: he turneth it whithersoever he will.

3. Proverbs 11:27 – He that diligently seeketh good procureth favour: but he that seeketh mischief, it shall come unto him.

4. Zechariah 12:10 – And I will pour upon the house of David, and upon the inhabitants of Jerusalem, the spirit of grace and of supplications: and they shall look upon me whom they have pierced, and they shall mourn for him, as one mourneth for his only son, and shall be in bitterness for him, as one that is in bitterness for his firstborn.

5. Philippians 4: 13,19 – [13] I can do all things through Christ which strengtheneth me....[19] But my God shall supply all your need according to his riches in glory by Christ Jesus.

EMPLOYMENT
PRAYER POINT: (PSALM 113:7-8)

- When you desire a job or when you have to interview for a new position. The provision of God for you as a born again and obedient child of God is to get the best things in this life and here after. God does not want His children to manage poverty. He desires to satisfy us with good things. As you confess and pray, every yoke of profitless hard work will be destroyed and God will give you profitable and long lasting employment.

EMPLOYMENT
CONFESSION OF PRAISE (SAY THIS ALOUD)

1. God, I thank You that You are God alone and You can advance me.
2. O' Lord, I thank You for bringing me into favor with everyone who will decide/make the final decision concerning my employment.
3. I reject the spirit of the tail and I claim the spirit of the head, in the name of Jesus.
4. I declare and decree that what is for me is for me and only me.
5. I receive the anointing to excel in the area of employment.

EMPLOYMENT
PRAYER:

Lord God,

I declare and decree that I am the head and not the tail. I'm above only and not beneath. I'm the lender and not the borrower. I declare that I've been elevated high above the nations of this Earth. I'm in position to receive the blessings of the Lord. Lord, catapult me into greatness as You did for Daniel in the land of Babylon. I bind every strongman delegated to hinder my progress in the name of Jesus. I dispatch Your angels to roll away every stumbling block that is sent to hinder my progress and block my employment, in Jesus name. I bind and render naught the spirit of strife, wrong words, demonic opinions, unprofitable controversies, evil collaborations, confusion and memory failure in the name of Jesus. I claim the position (call out the position you are applying for or desiring) in the mighty name of Jesus. Lord, hammer this matter into the minds of those who will be my coworkers and allow us to connect and work peacefully together. I declare that I have favor with the staff and there will be no hindrance concerning me and obtaining employment ever again, in Jesus name.

Praise & rejoice!
High praise & intensified prayer!

EMPLOYMENT

Prayer Request For Myself And Others:

1.
2.
3.
4.
5.
6.
7.
8.
9.
10.
11.
12.
13.
14.
15.
16.
17.
18.
19.
20.

Linda D. Law

EMPLOYMENT

Testimonial Page:

EMPLOYMENT

Gratitude and Answered Prayers :

Chapter 19

Hidden Curses

SCRIPTURES:

1. Galatians 3:13-14 – [13] Christ hath redeemed us from the curse of the law, being made a curse for us: for it is written, Cursed is every one that hangeth on a tree: [14] That the blessing of Abraham might come on the Gentiles through Jesus Christ; that we might receive the promise of the Spirit through faith.

2. Numbers 23:23 – Surely there is no enchantment against Jacob, neither is there any divination against Israel: according to this time it shall be said of Jacob and of Israel, What hath God wrought!

3. 2 Samuel 22:45-46 – [45] Strangers shall submit themselves unto me: as soon as they hear, they shall be obedient unto me. [46] Strangers shall fade away, and they shall be afraid out of their close places.

4. Proverbs 26:2 – As the bird by wandering, as the swallow by flying, so the curse causeless shall not come. (there has to be a reason)

5. Genesis 12:3 – And I will bless them that bless thee, and curse him that curseth thee: and in thee shall all families of the earth be blessed.

Linda D. Law

HIDDEN CURSES
PRAYER POINT: (2KINGS 2:18-22)

- This prayer, as well as this prayer point, is mainly used during deliverance of hidden curses that you may be presently dealing with. Many are laboring and functioning day to day under unexplainable burdens. In order to move forward there is an invisible barrier that has to be broken in the spirit. The heaven has become as brass and the Earth as iron. When some things seem not to be working, in spite of numerous efforts, there may be a hidden curse in place. We are in awe and thank God that Christ has redeemed us from the curse of the law. These confessions and prayers have been put in place to break hidden curses.

146

HIDDEN CURSES
CONFESSION OF PRAISE (SAY THIS ALOUD)

1. Praise the Lord for His redeeming power by the blood of Jesus.
2. Praise the Lord for redeeming us from the curse of the law.
3. I confess all sins that may have given the enemy a legal right to place any curse on me.
4. God, I thank You for forgiving and cleansing me from all unrighteousness.
5. I take authority over any and every curse in my life.

HIDDEN CURSES
PRAYER:

Lord God,

I thank You for Your forgiving power and I take complete authority over every curse upon my life. I command all curses issued against me to be broken in the name of Jesus. I command all evil spirits associated with any curse to leave my life, heart, and mind right now, in the name of Jesus. I take authority over generational curses and I command them to be broken. I take authority over inherited curses and I command them to be broken as well, in the name of Jesus. I take authority over curses arising from evil dedications, witchcraft, and word curses, conscious and unconscious wicked deeds. I break any curse which could possibly be in my parents' families back to 10 generations. I denounce and break any and all curses put on my family line as well as my descendants, in the name of Jesus. I cancel the consequences of all curses spoken over my life and I declare the root of my life is purged by the fire of the Holy Ghost, in the blessed name of Jesus. Allow the root of my life to be purged with the blood of Jesus. I break and cancel every curse placed on the children to punish their seed, in the name of Jesus. I cancel the curse that may have been placed on my very own parents or grandparents, even 100 generations back that would have an evil effect on my present life, in the name of Jesus. I reverse all curses and send them back to the sender. I declare curses shall be no more over my life in the name of Jesus.

Praise & rejoice!
High praise!
Intensified prayer!

HIDDEN CURSES

Prayer Request For Myself And Others:

1.
2.
3.
4.
5.
6.
7.
8.
9.
10.
11.
12.
13.
14.
15.
16.
17.
18.
19.
20.

Linda D. Law

HIDDEN CURSES

Testimonial Page:

HIDDEN CURSES

Gratitude and Answered Prayers :

Chapter 20

Divine Promotions

1. Psalm 75:6-7 – [6] For promotion cometh neither from the east, nor from the west, nor from the south. [7] But God is the judge: he putteth down one, and setteth up another.

2. James 4:10 – Humble yourselves in the sight of the Lord, and he shall lift you up.

3. Colossians 3:23 – And whatsoever ye do, do it heartily, as to the Lord, and not unto men;

4. Genesis 12:2 – And I will make of thee a great nation, and I will bless thee, and make thy name great; and thou shalt be a blessing:

5. Daniel 3:30 – Then the king promoted Shadrach, Meshach, and Abednego, in the province of Babylon.

DIVINE PROMOTIONS
PRAYER POINT: (MARK 10:46-52)

- When you desire divine promotion… If you could take on the attitude of the blind Bartimeus as he desperately cried out and help the attention of the Lord. You can be undoubtedly sure that your promotion will come. God is still in the blessing business of raising the less fortunate out of the valley and setting you among the princes of His people. Invite Jehovah El Roi into your situation and He will establish you among the people.

DIVINE PROMOTIONS
CONFESSION OF PRAISE (SAY THIS ALOUD)

1. I cut myself off from every territorial spirit, in the name of Jesus.
2. I rebuke the devourer in my life, in the name of Jesus.
3. Heal in me O' God, whatever needs to be healed.
4. Replace in me O' God, whatever needs to be replaced.
5. I command promotions to locate me in the spirit and elevate me, in Jesus name.

Linda D. Law

DIVINE PROMOTIONS
PRAYER:

Father God in the name of Jesus,

Let the fire of the Lord consume me and every dark place in my life, in the name of Jesus. I loosen myself from the bondage of profitless hard work and from the power of witchcraft and bewitchment that may have attached itself to my life through evil works spoken or evil deeds plotted against my life. I cancel the power of all curses upon my life and Satan. I close any and every door that I may have opened to you through ignorance and disobedience, in the name of Jesus. I bind the strongman over myself, my family, my blessings, my career, or anything and any person that's connected to me. I command the armor of the strongman to be burned by the fire of the Holy Ghost. I command total restoration and healing to take place in my life. I loosen myself from all inherited bondage. I command that any evil hand that's attempting to hold me from being promoted, be loosened and let go now, by the fire of the Holy Ghost. I declare and decree that every promotion that God has ordained and orchestrated for my life be released upon my life, in the matchless name of Jesus. I declare it all to be so, in the name of Jesus.

Praise & rejoice!
High praise & intensified prayer!

DIVINE PROMOTIONS

Prayer Request For Myself And Others:

1.
2.
3.
4.
5.
6.
7.
8.
9.
10.
11.
12.
13.
14.
15.
16.
17.
18.
19.
20.

Linda D. Law

DIVINE PROMOTIONS

Testimonial Page

DIVINE PROMOTIONS

Gratitude and Answered Prayers :

Chapter 21

Open Heavens

SCRIPTURES:

1. John 1:51 – And he saith unto him, Verily, verily, I say unto you, Hereafter ye shall see heaven open, and the angels of God ascending and descending upon the Son of man.

2. Isaiah 64:1 – Oh that thou wouldest rend the heavens, that thou wouldest come down, that the mountains might flow down at thy presence,

3. Psalm 113:5,7-8 – [5] Who is like unto the Lord our God, who dwelleth on high, [7] He raiseth up the poor out of the dust, and lifteth the needy out of the dunghill; [8]That he may set him with princes, even with the princes of his people.

4. Psalm 144:5-6 – [5] Bow thy heavens, O Lord, and come down: touch the mountains, and they shall smoke. [6]Cast forth lightning, and scatter them: shoot out thine arrows, and destroy them.

5. Ezekiel 1:1 – Now it came to pass in the thirtieth year, in the fourth month, in the fifth day of the month, as I was among the captives by the river of Chebar, that the heavens were opened, and I saw visions of God.

OPEN HEAVENS
PRAYER POINT: (GENESIS 28:17)

- Open heavens will enable us to obtain breakthroughs we need for our lives. When the heavens open the angels of God will begin to ascend and descend, bringing multiple blessings for the saints. These blessings include but aren't limited to favor, power, promotion, breakthroughs, financial gain, good health, sound mind, peace and much more. As you implement these confessions and prayers into your life, God will begin to ascend and descend upon your life.

OPEN HEAVENS

CONFESSION OF PRAISE (SAY THIS ALOUD)

1. O' Lord, thank You for making me Your good vessel.
2. I thank You that the windows of heaven are open concerning me.
3. I thank You that the windows of heaven are open concerning my assignment on this Earth.
4. I thank You that the windows of heaven are open concerning my finances, future, and faith.
5. I declare and I'm grateful that I'm in position to receive every blessing that's assigned to my life and I am indeed under an open heaven.

OPEN HEAVENS
PRAYER:

Father God,

Rend the heavens and please come down at my cry. Lord prepare me as a living and holy sanctuary for You. I declare every evil spirit working against me to be paralyzed and let the power from above fall on me to do the impossible, in the precious name of Jesus. Lord, let every good and perfect gift from above locate me today, in the name of Jesus. I boldly prophecy, in the name of Jesus, to every imperfect gift in my life… I command that they line up according to the perfect will of our Father. I command the rain of abundance, goodness; favor and mercy to fall on every department of my life and allow divine glory from above overshadow my life now, in the name of Jesus. I paralyze all enemies that stand against my open heavens and all powers that expand problems. I cancel and nullify any powers that delay miracles and I paralyze any and all destroyers of destiny, in the name of Jesus. Lord, consider me as a channel of your blessings in all areas of my life and allow my hands to be stronger than any and all opposing hands in Jesus name. Every stone of hindrance be rolled away, in Jesus name. I declare that anywhere I go I find favor and You God, have ordained me to do many exploits in my life. I declare and decree that I am under an open heaven and I will have everything God says is mine, in the mighty name of Jesus!

Praise & rejoice!
High praise & intensified prayer!

OPEN HEAVENS

Prayer Request For Myself And Others:

1.
2.
3.
4.
5.
6.
7.
8.
9.
10.
11.
12.
13.
14.
15.
16.
17.
18.
19.
20.

Linda D. Law

OPEN HEAVENS

Testimonial Page:

OPEN HEAVENS

Gratitude and Answered Prayers :

Chapter 22

Sick & Tired Of Being Sick & Tired

SCRIPTURES:

1. 1 Peter 4:3 – For the time past of our life may suffice us to have wrought the will of the Gentiles, when we walked in lasciviousness, lusts, excess of wine, revellings, banquetings, and abominable idolatries:

2. Philippians 4:13 – I can do all things through Christ which strengtheneth me.

3. Joshua 1:9 – Have not I commanded thee? Be strong and of a good courage; be not afraid, neither be thou dismayed: for the Lord thy God is with thee whithersoever thou goest.

4. Deuteronomy 31:6 – Be strong and of a good courage, fear not, nor be afraid of them: for the Lord thy God, he it is that doth go with thee; he will not fail thee, nor forsake thee.

5. Ephesians 6:10 – Finally, my brethren, be strong in the Lord, and in the power of his might.

Linda D. Law

SICK & TIRED OF BEING SICK & TIRED
PRAYER POINT: (1 PETER 4)

- We have to get to the point where we are willing to say, "I'm sick & tired of being sick & tired," or things will always remain the same. We have to be really dissatisfied with our situations before a change can come. In order to experience a change you first have to be willing to change. Therefore, if you aren't willing to change for the better you can bypass these confessions and prayers. A lot of our issues come directly from choices we have made due to lack of wisdom or immaturity. So let's make a change in our choices in order for a change to come in our lives.

SICK & TIRED OF BEING SICK & TIRED
CONFESSION OF PRAISE (SAY THIS ALOUD)

1. I'm thankful to God that I've come to the point that I am ready for a change.
2. I release myself from any and all strongholds and I declare myself free from the hand of the enemy.
3. I am willing, ready and able to move from where I am mentally, physically, and spiritually; to where God has destined me to be.
4. I shake off the spirit of slothfulness and laziness. I take authority over any demonic spirit that would attempt to hold me back.
5. I declare that I'm moving forward in every area of my life by the power of the Holy Ghost.

SICK & TIRED OF BEING SICK & TIRED
PRAYER:

Father God in the name of Jesus,

I command every satanic influence concerning my life to be rendered null and void, in the name of Jesus. I destroy the clock of the enemy for my life and I render his time for me to be up. I declare that every good thing that is dead must now come alive in my life. Healing power of God, overshadow me now, in Jesus name. I declare and decree that the spirit of procrastination, which lingers in my life, is no longer active. I declare that I'm energized by the power that God has given me. I am excited about the destiny He has set in front of me. I declare that I am no longer sitting around waiting for things to happen but by the mercy of God I'm allowing the Holy Spirit to guide me in making things happen. I silence the voice of the enemy and I paralyze his tricks, plots and plans that he's set to deter me from walking in places and connecting with people. I am now obtaining things that God predestined for my life before the foundation of this world was set. I declare and decree that I am in a different space and a different place in my life. What the enemy designed for my bad, God has determined it to be for my good! In the name of Jesus I do pray. Amen.

Praise & rejoice!
High praise & intensified prayer!

SICK & TIRED OF BEING SICK & TIRED

Prayer Request For Myself And Others:

1.
2.
3.
4.
5.
6.
7.
8.
9.
10.
11.
12.
13.
14.
15.
16.
17.
18.
19.
20.

Linda D. Law

SICK & TIRED OF BEING SICK & TIRED

Testimonial Page:

174

SICK & TIRED OF BEING SICK & TIRED

Gratitude and Answered Prayers :

Chapter 23

Deliverance From Religion

SCRIPTURES:

1. Matthew 7:21 – Not every one that saith unto me, Lord, Lord, shall enter into the kingdom of heaven; but he that doeth the will of my Father which is in heaven.

2. John 14:6 – JJesus saith unto him, I am the way, the truth, and the life: no man cometh unto the Father, but by me.

3. Isaiah 52:2 – Shake thyself from the dust; arise, and sit down, O Jerusalem: loose thyself from the bands of thy neck, O captive daughter of Zion.

4. Galatians 6:6 – Let him that is taught in the word communicate unto him that teacheth in all good things.

5. Revelation 2:7 – He that hath an ear, let him hear what the Spirit saith unto the churches; To him that overcometh will I give to eat of the tree of life, which is in the midst of the paradise of God.

Linda D. Law

DELIVERANCE FROM RELIGION
PRAYER POINT: (2 CORINTHIANS 11:3-4)

- A religious spirit is a type of demonic spirit that influences a person or a group of people to replace a genuine relationship with God with works and traditions. When you operate out of a religious spirit you attempt to earn salvation. As believers, we must desire an authentic relationship with our Father. By making these confessions and praying from a genuine and pure place, God will deliver you from religious ties. Just believe it!

DELIVERANCE FROM RELIGION
CONFESSION OF PRAISE (SAY THIS ALOUD)

1. God, I confess that I held on to some resentment and bitterness that may have attached me to the spirit of religion.
2. I know now that this is a sin and I confess it as such. I believe because I have confessed it as a sin. God is faithful and just enough to forgive me.
3. I denounce all contacts that I may have had with religious spirits and I declare that I am free.
4. I close any and every door that may have opened to the spirit of religion out of ignorance.
5. I declare that I am free in my mind, body and spirit. I am now open to allow the Holy Spirit to guide me in all truths.

Linda D. Law

DELIVERANCE FROM RELIGION
PRAYER:

Father God in the name of Jesus,

I claim victory over my life in every area. God, I confess all of my sins and I denounce all contacts that I've had with religious spirits. I denounce the spirit of pride, the spirit of manipulation, the spirit of manmade religion and religious spirits. I declare and decree that I am totally separated from these things that pull me away from an authentic relationship with God, my Father. Satan, I rebuke you and I close any and all doors which I or even my ancestors may have opened to you, in the name of Jesus. I break each and every curse of family destruction. I release myself from the hold of any religious spirits and I command them to release the hold off of my life, in the name of Jesus. I break the spirit of false compassion, selfishness, fear of poverty, guilt and unworthiness off of my life. I declare, by the power of the Holy Ghost, that I am free and I loosen myself from the spirit that intends to destroy my life. I declare that I am free from any religious spirits. I thank God that I will never entangle myself in this another day of my life. God, I thank You for freeing me, because He who the Son sets free is free indeed. I bless You father, in Jesus name.

Praise & rejoice!
High praise & intensified prayers!

DELIVERANCE FROM RELIGION

Prayer Request For Myself And Others:

1.
2.
3.
4.
5.
6.
7.
8.
9.
10.
11.
12.
13.
14.
15.
16.
17.
18.
19.
20.

Linda D. Law

DELIVERANCE FROM RELIGION

Testimonial Page:

DELIVERANCE FROM RELIGION

Gratitude and Answered Prayers :

Chapter 24

Breaking Negative Flow

SCRIPTURES:

1. 1 John 5:19 – And we know that we are of God, and the whole world lieth in wickedness.

2. 1 Kings 14:9 – But hast done evil above all that were before thee: for thou hast gone and made thee other gods, and molten images, to provoke me to anger, and hast cast me behind thy back:

3. 1 Peter 3:9 – Not rendering evil for evil, or railing for railing: but contrariwise blessing; knowing that ye are thereunto called, that ye should inherit a blessing.

4. 1 Samuel 12:20 – And Samuel said unto the people, Fear not: ye have done all this wickedness: yet turn not aside from following the Lord, but serve the Lord with all your heart;

5. 2 Chronicles 29:6 – For our fathers have trespassed, and done that which was evil in the eyes of the Lord our God, and have forsaken him, and have turned away their faces from the habitation of the Lord, and turned their backs.

BREAKING NEGATIVE FLOW
PRAYER POINT: (NUMBERS 23)

- When we accept Jesus Christ as our Lord and Savior, we automatically receive the power to break yokes and destroy evil flow. The bible states, "But as many as received him, to them gave the power to become sons of God, even to them that believe on his name." This clearly means that every evil flow in your life has to be cut off and destroyed by the power of the Holy Ghost, in order that you can go with ease in the spirit of God. Every generational curse or ancestral curse has to break. In this section of prayer we will break every flow of evil that's flowing freely in your life.

BREAKING NEGATIVE FLOW
CONFESSION OF PRAISE (SAY THIS ALOUD)

1. I confess that I am a child of God.
2. I confess that I am saved and I possess all possessions afforded me in Christ Jesus.
3. I confess that I do not repay evil with evil however I repay evil with good when it's in my power to do so.
4. I confess that even though I've done evil in my days, I serve a God of grace. He forgives my sins and frees me from the curse of the enemy.
5. I confess that though I am born of man and woman, I am not attached to their lives. I am free from the curse of the law.

BREAKING NEGATIVE FLOW
PRAYER:

God,

I thank You for making the necessary detachment from any and every kind of bondage. I release myself from any issue given into my life before birth. I break and loose myself from every generational curse, in the name of Jesus. I break and loose myself by the fire of the Holy Ghost from every inherited disorder in my body, whether it is known or unknown. I break all curses of poverty, deformity, and sickness that are connected to my life. I pray this prayer over anyone that's divinely connected to me or my family, in the name of Jesus. I declare God will arise and cause every evil force to be scattered. Every mind controlling and manipulating spirit will burn by the fire of the Holy Ghost. I declare and decree the spirit of death and hell to lose its grip and surrender its hold on my life. I reject every evil word spoken over my life that is attempting to redirect my destiny. Evil has absolutely no place in my life and I set fire to every trick, plot and plan that the enemy has set to trip me. I denounce and burn it. I call it to be null and void over my life, in the name of Jesus.

Praise & rejoice!
High praise & intensified prayer!

BREAKING NEGATIVE FLOW

Prayer Request For Myself And Others:

1.
2.
3.
4.
5.
6.
7.
8.
9.
10.
11.
12.
13.
14.
15.
16.
17.
18.
19.
20.

Linda D. Law

BREAKING NEGATIVE FLOW

Testimonial Page:

BREAKING NEGATIVE FLOW

Gratitude and Answered Prayers :

Chapter 25

Deliverance For Children

SCRIPTURES:

1. Luke 1:41 – And it came to pass, that, when Elisabeth heard the salutation of Mary, the babe leaped in her womb; and Elisabeth was filled with the Holy Ghost:

2. Psalm 139:13 –For thou hast possessed my reins: thou hast covered me in my mother's womb.

3. Isaiah 44:2 – Thus saith the Lord that made thee, and formed thee from the womb, which will help thee; Fear not, O Jacob, my servant; and thou, Jesurun, whom I have chosen.

4. Galatians 1:15 – But when it pleased God, who separated me from my mother's womb, and called me by his grace,

5. Jeremiah 1:5 – Before I formed thee in the belly I knew thee; and before thou camest forth out of the womb I sanctified thee, and I ordained thee a prophet unto the nations.

DELIVERANCE FOR CHILDREN
PRAYER POINT: (MARK 10:14-16)

- I'm not sure what your child needs deliverance from; whether it's one thing or multiple things. I do know that one touch from our Lord and Savior Christ Jesus can solve every issue. Here, we want you to simply invite Jesus into whatever the situation might be and ask Him to take control. All children need to be prayed for in a very serious manner, especially in these days and times. They are constantly and consistently placed under the protection of the blood of Jesus. Here we will bind and break every evil curse or evil word spoken over your child(ren). Your seed will walk in the power of the Most High, in Jesus name!

DELIVERANCE FOR CHILDREN
CONFESSION OF PRAISE (SAY THIS ALOUD)

1. Thank You God for giving me the blessing of having a child(ren).
2. God, thank You for making my child(ren) great before You. You will do great exploits through my children.
3. I thank You that no sickness, plague, infectious disease or virus will come upon my children.
4. I thank You for health, wholeness and soundness of mind concerning my children.
5. God, I thank You that my child(ren) will not/has not inherited any evil spirit or generational curse in Jesus name.

DELIVERANCE FOR CHILDREN
PRAYER:

O' God,

I thank You that my child(ren) will be saved at an early age. I declare that as my child(ren) mature he/she will also mature in the things of God. I cover my child(ren) with the blood of Jesus and surround them by a divine hedge of protection, in the name of Jesus. I declare my child(ren) are healthy, wealthy and he/she prospers even as his/her soul prospers. I declare my son/daughters digestive, respiratory, and circulatory systems are normal, strong and healthy. I declare my child(ren) blood is flowing as it should and it's free from any infections or anything related to blood disorders, in the precious name of Jesus. God, I cut off any and every evil flow of hereditary problems in Jesus name. I bind and break every evil and negative ancestral spirit. Spirit of witchcraft, generational curse and every evil thing I command it to lose its hold on my child(ren), in the name of Jesus. I command anything that would possibly prevent my child from being a blessing in their life or the life of others, to be burned and shattered by the fire of the Holy Ghost. Father, I thank You that no weapon formed against my child(ren) shall prosper and every tongue that rises against him/her in judgment shall be condemned. I declare this all to be so, in the name of Jesus.

Praise & rejoice!
High praise & intensified prayer!

DELIVERANCE FOR CHILDREN

Prayer Request For Myself And Others:

1.
2.
3.
4.
5.
6.
7.
8.
9.
10.
11.
12.
13.
14.
15.
16.
17.
18.
19.
20.

Linda D. Law

DELIVERANCE FOR CHILDREN

Testimonial Page:

DELIVERANCE FOR CHILDREN

Gratitude and Answered Prayers :

Chapter 26

Healing

SCRIPTURES:

1. Isaiah 53:4-5 – [4] Surely he hath borne our griefs, and carried our sorrows: yet we did esteem him stricken, smitten of God, and afflicted. [5] But he was wounded for our transgressions, he was bruised for our iniquities: the chastisement of our peace was upon him; and with his stripes we are healed.

2. Jeremiah 30:17 – For I will restore health unto thee, and I will heal thee of thy wounds, saith the Lord; because they called thee an Outcast, saying, This is Zion, whom no man seeketh after.

3. Deuteronomy 32:39 – See now that I, even I, am he, and there is no god with me: I kill, and I make alive; I wound, and I heal: neither is there any that can deliver out of my hand.

4. 2 Chronicles 7:14 – If my people, which are called by my name, shall humble themselves, and pray, and seek my face, and turn from their wicked ways; then will I hear from heaven, and will forgive their sin, and will heal their land.

5. Isaiah 38:16-17 – [16] O Lord, by these things men live, and in all these things is the life of my spirit: so wilt thou recover me, and make me to live. [17] Behold, for peace I had great bitterness: but thou hast in love to my soul delivered it from the pit of corruption: for thou hast cast all my sins behind thy back.

HEALING
PRAYER POINT: (ISAIAH 53:5)

- Healing is still real today and you must know it! Of course Jesus is not here in the physical to heal however he uses people of faith like you and I. As long as you have accepted Jesus Christ as your Lord and Savior, the power to heal is flowing through your hands. The bible states that we will lay hands on the sick and they will recover. We have to believe that by the blood of Jesus we are free from any sickness or any infectious disease or viruses. Our confessions and prayers will allow us to believe healing concerning others as we also ask for ourselves.

HEALING

CONFESSION OF PRAISE (SAY THIS ALOUD)

1. I have the power to heal because I am a blood bought believer.
2. I am healed by the blood of Jesus from all sicknesses and diseases.
3. O' Lord, my God, I cried unto thee and thou hast healed me.
4. Many are the afflictions of the righteous but God will deliver me out of them all.
5. I am forgiven from all of my iniquities and He who heals all of my diseases has washed me clean.

Linda D. Law

HEALING
Prayer:

God,

I thank You for Your mighty power that is more than able to heal sickness and diseases. Thank You God for being the God that heals me and others. Let Your healing hands be stretched out upon my life now, in the precious name of Jesus. You are Jehovah Rapha - the Lord who heals. Let Your healing power fill this place. May all the enemies of my health be scattered, in the name of Jesus. Heal me, O' God, and I will be healed. Father God, save me from the deadly pestilence that lives in darkness and release me from the clutch of the enemy and cause me to enjoy good health. Cover me with your wings and help me to find healing and wholeness in Your love. Lord, I pray that in my spirit of heaviness that I put on the garment of praise. I pray that I will not wallow in my pain or in my sickness. Instead, allow my mind to be fixated on lifting You up. I silence the mouth of my enemies concerning my health. I prosper even as my soul prospers. God, I thank You that the enemies plan concerning my health is null and void. Heavenly father I thank You, that no weapon formed against my health shall prosper. I decree I walk in total health and healing in Jesus name.

Praise & rejoice!
High praise & intensified prayer!

HEALING

Prayer Request For Myself And Others:

1.
2.
3.
4.
5.
6.
7.
8.
9.
10.
11.
12.
13.
14.
15.
16.
17.
18.
19.
20.

Linda D. Law

HEALING

Testimonial Page:

HEALING

Gratitude and Answered Prayers :

Chapter 27

Destiny Destroyers

SCRIPTURES:

1. 1 Corinthians 2:7- 8 – [7] But we speak the wisdom of God in a mystery, even the hidden wisdom, which God ordained before the world unto our glory: [8] Which none of the princes of this world knew: for had they known it, they would not have crucified the Lord of glory.

2. Obadiah 1:17 – But upon mount Zion shall be deliverance, and there shall be holiness; and the house of Jacob shall possess their possessions.

3. Malachi 3:6 – For I am the Lord, I change not; therefore ye sons of Jacob are not consumed.

4. Romans 8:28 – And we know that all things work together for good to them that love God, to them who are the called according to his purpose.

5. Isaiah 54:17 – No weapon that is formed against thee shall prosper; and every tongue that shall rise against thee in judgment thou shalt condemn. This is the heritage of the servants of the Lord, and their righteousness is of me, saith the Lord.

DESTINY DESTROYERS

PRAYER POINT: (2CORINTHIANS 10:3-6)

- The weapons of our warfare are not carnal but are mighty through the pulling down of strongholds. Warfare weapons are the most powerful. They can destroy all attacks aimed for your destiny. They destroy those word curses of those that are attempting to hinder you from getting to your appointed place. The bible states the power of life and death is in your mouth. You must use the powerful word of God that will resurrect your destiny. You must pray for those that despitefully use you. We call them "haters" in today's world. If we use our haters to our advantage we will be elevated during their little attacks. We will learn through confessions and prayers how to cause those alleged destiny destroyers to work for us! Let's do this!

DESTINY DESTROYERS

CONFESSION OF PRAISE (SAY THIS ALOUD)

1. I declare that my divine destiny will appear and the perverted destiny will disappear.
2. All evil power that has a negative influence over my destiny will be made impotent.
3. Any damage done to my destiny, I declare it repaired, in Jesus name.
4. I declare the enemy will not convert my destiny to be one of failure and disappointments.
5. I command by the power of the Holy Ghost that all darkness assigned to my destiny leave and never return.

DESTINY DESTROYERS
PRAYER:

Father in the name of Jesus,

Let my divine destiny appear and allow perverted destiny to disappear. I reject all satanic realignment of my destiny from prospering. I refuse to live below my divine standards and I ask You God to restore me to my original design for my life, in the name of Jesus. I reject anything that's working against my life and I declare the spirit of excellence to come upon me. Satan, I remove from you the right to rob me of my destiny. I command all powers of darkness, assigned to my destiny to leave and never return, in the name of Jesus. I command all the enemies of Christ Jesus that have access to my progress, to leave and never return. I paralyze any satanic opportunities coming against my life. I render null and void the influence of destiny destroyers, which are those that come against my life, as well as Gods will for my life. I refuse to be removed from the divine agenda, in Jesus name. I break every evil diversion in Jesus name. I command anything that has attached itself to my life through evil words spoken and witchcraft to be burned by the fire of the Holy Ghost. I declare this all to be so, in the name of Jesus.

Praise & rejoice!
High praise & intensified prayer!

DESTINY DESTROYERS

Prayer Request For Myself And Others:

1.
2.
3.
4.
5.
6.
7.
8.
9.
10.
11.
12.
13.
14.
15.
16.
17.
18.
19.
20.

Linda D. Law

DESTINY DESTROYERS

Testimonial Page:

DESTINY DESTROYERS

Gratitude and Answered Prayers :

Chapter 28

Defeating Defeat

SCRIPTURES:

1. Colossians 2:15 – And having spoiled principalities and powers, he made a shew of them openly, triumphing over them in it.

2. John 16:33 – These things I have spoken unto you, that in me ye might have peace. In the world ye shall have tribulation: but be of good cheer; I have overcome the world.

3. Psalm 118:10-11 – [10] All nations compassed me about: but in the name of the Lord will I destroy them. [11] They compassed me about; yea, they compassed me about: but in the name of the Lord I will destroy them.

4. Psalm 91:1-4 – [1] He that dwelleth in the secret place of the most High shall abide under the shadow of the Almighty. [2] I will say of the Lord, He is my refuge and my fortress: my God; in him will I trust. [3] Surely he shall deliver thee from the snare of the fowler, and from the noisome pestilence. [4] He shall cover thee with his feathers, and under his wings shalt thou trust: his truth shall be thy shield and buckler.

5. James 4:7 – Submit yourselves therefore to God. Resist the devil, and he will flee from you.

DEFEATING DEFEAT
PRAYER POINT: (JUDGES 6)

- How do we defeat, defeat? We defeat it by tapping into the greatest power that has ever been recorded in history. The cross is where the devil planned to use what looked like an opportunity, to defeat Jesus. However, Satan suffered his greatest loss. Jesus actually stripped the devil and his imps of their powers to condemn and kill the human race. Jesus said these things have I spoken to you who are in the world. We will have tribulation but be of a good heart. I have overcome the world. These confessions and prayers will cause you to defeat every life issue that's attempting to defeat you. You have the victory!

DEFEATING DEFEAT
CONFESSION OF PRAISE (SAY THIS ALOUD)

1. I declare victory over any power sponsoring demotion and any kind of embarrassment against me or my destiny.
2. I declare and decree that the devil is defeated in my life.
3. I say all of my enemies will surrender in shame.
4. Every trick, plot and plan the enemy has plotted against my life is declared null and void/powerless.
5. I declare I am the head and not the tail, above only and not beneath. I'm a lender and not a borrower!!! I am not defeated!

DEFEATING DEFEAT
PRAYER:

Father God in the name of Jesus,

I cancel every spiritual transaction that's working against my life to be rendered dead, in the name of Jesus. I declare that anything in my life opening the door to the enemy must go back to the sender. I command all of my enemies to surrender and be led away by the power of the Holy Ghost, in the name of Jesus. Angels of the living God recover my stolen blessings and any good thing in my life placed on any evil mind, so that it is withdrawn in the name of Jesus. O' Lord, please amaze me by Your signs and wonders while burying every doubt that may surface in my life, in Jesus name. God, let every seed of poverty in the foundation of my life fall down and die instantly, in the name of Jesus. I detach myself from the hands of the enemy and I command that it loose its hold, in the name of Jesus. I declare and decree that no weapon that's formed against me shall prosper and every tongue that rises against me in judgment shall be condemned. The devil is defeated and his power is useless in my life. I am victorious and nothing that the enemy can or will do can hinder me from moving forward. Defeat was defeated at the cross and therefore I am victorious.

Praise & rejoice!
High praise & intensified prayer!

DEFEATING DEFEAT

Prayer Request For Myself And Others:

1.
2.
3.
4.
5.
6.
7.
8.
9.
10.
11.
12.
13.
14.
15.
16.
17.
18.
19.
20.

Linda D. Law

DEFEATING DEFEAT

Testimonial Page:

DEFEATING DEFEAT

Gratitude and Answered Prayers :

Chapter 29

Spirit Of Fear

SCRIPTURES:

1. 2 Timothy 1:7 – For God hath not given us the spirit of fear; but of power, and of love, and of a sound mind.

2. Philippians 4:6-7 – 6 Be careful for nothing; but in every thing by prayer and supplication with thanksgiving let your requests be made known unto God. 7 And the peace of God, which passeth all understanding, shall keep your hearts and minds through Christ Jesus.

3. 1 John 4:18 – There is no fear in love; but perfect love casteth out fear: because fear hath torment. He that feareth is not made perfect in love.

4. Romans 8:26 – Likewise the Spirit also helpeth our infirmities: for we know not what we should pray for as we ought: but the Spirit itself maketh intercession for us with groanings which cannot be uttered.

5. Hebrews 13:6 – So that we may boldly say, The Lord is my helper, and I will not fear what man shall do unto me.

SPIRIT OF FEAR
PRAYER POINT: (JOB 3:25)

- God wishes above all things that you prosper and be in good health, even as your soul prospers. Therefore, every evil spirit of fear must reverse and get out of your life. Fear has paralyzed us in so many areas of our lives and has caused us to prematurely abort the vision that God has for our lives. Fear has gripped us in our finances, faith and our future. After acknowledging God's word over your life and praying the prayer of faith, by your faith and confessions, the spirit of fear will be lifted off of your life.

SPIRIT OF FEAR

CONFESSION OF PRAISE (SAY THIS ALOUD)

1. In the name of Jesus, I refuse to fear because God has not given me the spirit of fear.
2. I am loosed from the grip of my past hurts, disappointments and fears.
3. The evil that I've observed in my family's background will not cause me to fear that my life will be cursed due to it.
4. Spirit of fear, lose your hold upon my life and the lives of my family members.
5. I command all humans using the spirit of fear to terrify me and cause me to stumble and fall, be removed, in Jesus name.

SPIRIT OF FEAR
PRAYER:

Father God in the name of Jesus,

I refuse to fear because God has not given me the spirit of fear, but of power and of love and of a sound mind. I bind the spirit of fear in my life. I declare every power, behind every activity of fear in my life, receive the wrath of God and be consumed by the fire of the Holy Ghost. The failures and disappointments of my past will not manifest in any area of my life, in the name of Jesus. I declare and decree that the fear of not being spiritually fulfilled will not spread throughout my life. The fear of not being able to overcome weaknesses; I command it to lose its hold, in the name of Jesus. I bind and cast down every fear of compromising and losing my faith, my salvation, and the fear of losing the anointing to be bound and destroyed, in the name of Jesus. I declare and decree that I am loosed completely from the spirit of fear in every area of my life, in the name of Jesus!

Praise & rejoice!
High praise & intensified prayer!

SPIRIT OF FEAR

Prayer Request For Myself And Others:

1.
2.
3.
4.
5.
6.
7.
8.
9.
10.
11.
12.
13.
14.
15.
16.
17.
18.
19.
20.

Linda D. Law

SPIRIT OF FEAR

Testimonial Page:

SPIRIT OF FEAR

Gratitude and Answered Prayers :

.

Chapter 30

Sexual Perversion

SCRIPTURES:

1. Ephesians 5:3-4 – ³ But fornication, and all uncleanness, or covetousness, let it not be once named among you, as becometh saints; ⁴ Neither filthiness, nor foolish talking, nor jesting, which are not convenient: but rather giving of thanks.

2. Proverbs 12:8 – A man shall be commended according to his wisdom: but he that is of a perverse heart shall be despised.

3. Ezekiel 9:9 –Then said he unto me, The iniquity of the house of Israel and Judah is exceeding great, and the land is full of blood, and the city full of perverseness: for they say, The Lord hath forsaken the earth, and the Lord seeth not.

4. Matthew 17:17 – Then Jesus answered and said, O faithless and perverse generation, how long shall I be with you? how long shall I suffer you? bring him hither to me.

5. Proverbs 19:3 – The foolishness of man perverteth his way: and his heart fretteth against the Lord.

SEXUAL PERVERSION
PRAYER POINT: (ROMANS 6:14)

- Sexual sins often open the doors to all kinds of evil spirits to enter. Is your desire is to be delivered from the spiritual contamination resulting from past or present sexual sins? Those that want to be delivered from their present sexual lusts, enticement and other sexual sins... Don't worry because you will be lifted up to the height of purity which God has called you to. As you confess and pray sincerely with a contrite/repentant heart, God will set you free from the chains of sexual perversion. Satan will lose his grip off of your life.

SEXUAL PERVERSION
CONFESSION OF PRAISE (SAY THIS ALOUD)

1. Thank You God for Your power to deliver me from any and every bondage.
2. I thank You God that I've been broken from every spirit of sexual perversion.
3. I release myself from every spirit of sexual sin from my past, including sins of fornication and sexual immorality, in Jesus name.
4. I declare and command every spirit of sexual perversion working against my life to be paralyzed, in Jesus name.
5. I declare that every demon of sexual perversion assigned to my life be bound, in Jesus name.

SEXUAL PERVERSION
PRAYER:

God,

I thank You for Your power to be delivered from sexual bondage. I break myself from every spirit of sexual perversion, in the name of Jesus. I release myself from every spirit that has attached itself to my life from my past connections. Father God, let the power of sexual perversion oppressing my life be burned by the fire of the Holy Ghost. May each and every inherited demon of sexual perversion in my life receive arrows of fire and be bound permanently, in Jesus name. God, I command every demonic stronghold built in my life, by the spirit of sexual perversion, to be cast down and burned in the name of Jesus. God, please allow my soul to be delivered from the forces of sexual perversion. I break the hold of this sin of perversion over my life and I nullify every effect of sexual perversion! Holy Ghost fire, purge my life completely, in the name of Jesus. God, I thank You for what the enemy meant for my bad, will work for my good. I denounce the spirit of lust and any other perverted spirit that has caused me to be hindered in my walk with Christ Jesus. I declare and decree that I'm no longer bound by the hand of the enemy. His grip is loosed and I'm no longer under attack in my heart, mind, body, soul or spirit. In the name of Jesus, I declare it all to be so!

Praise & rejoice!
High praise & intensified prayer!

SEXUAL PERVERSION

Prayer Request For Myself And Others:

1.
2.
3.
4.
5.
6.
7.
8.
9.
10.
11.
12.
13.
14.
15.
16.
17.
18.
19.
20.

Linda D. Law

SEXUAL PERVERSION

Testimonial Page:

SEXUAL PERVERSION

Gratitude and Answered Prayers :

About the Author

And we know that ALL things work together for the good of them that loves the Lord those that are the called according to His purpose. Linda Law has faced many challenges in life. However the promise that IT'S ALL GOOD has actually saved her life. When it seemed like she had nothing to hold on to she held on to that one promise!

Linda is an author of 3 published books entitled *Roller Coaster Ride to Destiny*, *Working Gods Plan* and *Praying During A Pandemic*. She is an entrepreneur with successful businesses in childcare around the state of Alabama where she was born & raised. Linda is a graduate of Bluewater Massage Institute and is a Certified Massage Therapist. Linda is a veteran of the US Army and graduate of University of Louisville. She is also a member of the Alpha Kappa Alpha Sorority (Beta Epsilon).

Through every challenge, every hardship, God kept saying KEEP PUSHING and that's what she's doing! God has called her to minister to those that are broken, discouraged and those that simply need a word that will thrust them into their NEXT all across the globe. Her ability to keep moving forward despite obstacles comes from the desire to leave a legacy and a heritage for her family generations to come. Her encouragement comes from the word knowing all things work together for her good in real life! Keep trusting, keep believing & keep moving forward.

www.ingramcontent.com/pod-product-compliance
Lightning Source LLC
Chambersburg PA
CBHW070346090426
42733CB00009B/1307